Crowdsourcing in Higher Edu

Significant disruption to the educational sector occurred due to the COVID-19 pandemic. This shed light on the need for new delivery methods and greater collaboration, which has become urgent and obvious as existing structures and traditional channels have struggled to cope or shut down. Higher education institutions often fail to crowdsource successfully because crowds differ in how they are organized compared to traditional sourcing. Instead of managing, higher education institutions work with external contributors who self-select into the process.

Crowdsourcing has significant potential to transform the education space by enhancing existing methodologies and offering innovative possibilities to develop new pedagogical techniques. This offers benefits for practitioners, institutions, students and participants. Drawing on theory and best practice, illustrated with a wide range of the examples and cases, *Crowdsourcing for Innovation in Higher Education* offers invaluable guidance and will be of interest to researchers, academics, policymakers, and students in the fields of higher education, development studies, organizational studies, management science and knowledge management.

Regina Lenart-Gansiniec is Associate Professor at the Department of Management of Higher Education Institutions at Jagiellonian University, Cracow, Poland.

Łukasz Sułkowski is Professor and Head of the Department of Management of Higher Education Institutions at Jagiellonian University, Cracow, Poland, President of PCG Poland and Vice-Rector of Academy WSB from Dabrowa Gornicza, Poland.

Routledge Advances in Management and Business Studies

Family Business and Management
Objectives, Theory, and Practice
Magdalena Biel and Beata Ślusarczyk

Consumer Packaging Strategy
Localisation in Asian Markets
Huda Khan, Richard Lee and Polymeros Chrysochou

Distress Risk and Corporate Failure Modelling
The State of the Art
Stewart Jones

Collaborative Leadership and Innovation
Management, Strategy and Creativity
Elis Carlström

Crowdsourcing for Innovation in Higher Education
Regina Lenart-Gansiniec and Łukasz Sułkowski

The Corporation of the Future
Edited by Stuart Orr and Paul Hunter

Organizational Management and the COVID-19 Crisis
Security and Risk Management Dilemmas
Edited by Wioletta Sylwia Wereda, Jacek Woźniak and Justyna Stochaj

Digital Entrepreneurship and the Global Economy
Edited by J. Mark Munoz

For more information about this series, please visit: www.routledge.com/Routledge-Advances-in-Management-and-Business-Studies/book-series/SE0305

Crowdsourcing for Innovation in Higher Education

Regina Lenart-Gansiniec
and Łukasz Sułkowski

NEW YORK AND LONDON

First published 2023
by Routledge
605 Third Avenue, New York, NY 10158

and by Routledge
4 Park Square, Milton Park, Abingdon, Oxon, OX14 4RN

Routledge is an imprint of the Taylor & Francis Group, an informa business

© 2023 Regina Lenart-Gansiniec and Łukasz Sułkowski

The right of Regina Lenart-Gansiniec and Łukasz Sułkowski to be identified as authors of this work has been asserted in accordance with sections 77 and 78 of the Copyright, Designs and Patents Act 1988.

This project was financed from the funds provided by the National Science Centre, Poland awarded on the basis of decision number DEC-2019/35/B/HS4/01446.

All rights reserved. No part of this book may be reprinted or reproduced or utilised in any form or by any electronic, mechanical, or other means, now known or hereafter invented, including photocopying and recording, or in any information storage or retrieval system, without permission in writing from the publishers.

Trademark notice: Product or corporate names may be trademarks or registered trademarks, and are used only for identification and explanation without intent to infringe.

Library of Congress Cataloging-in-Publication Data
A catalog record for this title has been requested

ISBN: 978-1-032-12996-9 (hbk)
ISBN: 978-1-032-13000-2 (pbk)
ISBN: 978-1-003-22717-5 (ebk)

DOI: 10.4324/9781003227175

Typeset in Bembo
by KnowledgeWorks Global Ltd.

Contents

Introduction   1

1 The Changing Context of Crowdsourcing in the Higher Education: Digital Transformation   4
ŁUKASZ SUŁKOWSKI

2 Digital Innovations: A New Direction for Higher Education   32
REGINA LENART-GANSINIEC

3 Crowdsourcing and What's Next?   48
REGINA LENART-GANSINIEC

4 Boosting Innovation of Higher Education Institutions with Crowdsourcing   70
REGINA LENART-GANSINIEC

5 Innovations in Knowledge Through Crowdsourcing   80
ŁUKASZ SUŁKOWSKI

6 How Crowdsourcing Is Changing Innovation: Perspective Post-COVID HEI's   95
ŁUKASZ SUŁKOWSKI

Conclusion   109

Index   112

Introduction

For some time now, higher education has been subject to a series of fundamental challenges, such as an increase in the world-wide competition, a decrease in financial resources and funding, as well as a more general questioning of its broader societal role and overall mission. In the face of a high level of changeability of the school environment (also in the context of higher education institutions [HEIs]), democratization of public life, pressure from multiple stakeholders, the need for effective actions, transparency, openness and professionalization of management – these organizations are forced to change the way and logic of action. This puts new challenges ahead of the decision-makers, which leads to the need to look for solutions that enable achievement of the above objectives. To compete in today's rapidly changing business environment, the HEI must constantly improve its current offering by creating new services to better meet changing requirements of its customers. To meet this need for continuous innovation, HEIs open their innovation processes to ideas and suggestions from various parties beyond their organizational boundaries, such as their suppliers, customers and even competitors.

In recent years, both theory and practice of management indicate that this is possible due to organizational changes, school organizations gaining access to unique, external intangible assets, increase in adaptability, taking pre-emptive and proactive action, transparency, accountability, openness and including the largest number of people who are interested in shaping and improving the strategic processes of the organization. With the continuing increase in the use of online distributed learning environments, crowdsourcing for education is becoming more important. Crowdsourcing refers to the activity of outsourcing a task to a large, undefined "crowd" (an organization, an informal or formal team, or individuals). In particular, crowdsourcing develops innovation education with large-scale learning resources, state-of-the-practice activities, flexible and personalized support, and more accurate and diverse feedbacks.

There are many reasons why organizations use crowdsourcing. Firstly, the use of crowdsourcing enables access to talent, external knowledge, valuable information, resources, skills and experience, mobilization and

DOI: 10.4324/9781003227175-1

competences. This can contribute to organizational learning, the organization's openness to new external knowledge. Secondly, crowdsourcing facilitates acquisition of not only new ideas, but also ways to solve problems or create innovation. Thirdly, there is also some potential of crowdsourcing in terms of building a competitive advantage, improving business processes, optimizing the costs of an organization's operations or business models. Fourthly, crowdsourcing is helpful in crisis management, expanding the current activity and offer of the organization, strategic planning, creating the image of the organization and improving communication with the environment.

There is some conviction among crowdsourcing promoters in HEIs that it can be useful for gaining ideas, opinions, feedback from the virtual community, gaining support for various projects, as well as improving communication between individual stakeholders, and even collecting data as part of scientific research, creating textbooks and raising funds for educational projects. In the case of the latter, it is indicated that the use of crowdsourcing enables optimization of the institution's budget and a more effective use of time for learning.

With the continuing increase in the use of online distributed learning environments, crowdsourcing of educational research efforts is becoming more important. Crowdsourcing is a new paradigm of educational technology development over the next few years. There are some books dealing with crowdsourcing. However there are no publications dealing with crowdsourcing in higher education. Therefore, there is a need for practitioners and academics to further explore the innovative use of crowdsourcing in education. Crowdsourcing in higher education differs in individual cases in terms of scale, coverage and type. Nevertheless, it can be indicated that all types of crowdsourcing are implemented at universities: from collective intelligence to value creation by the crowd, to gathering opinions and raising funds, with the predominance of crowdfunding projects and those related to collecting analytical data. Crowdsourcing in higher education, according to the information provided by the initiators of crowdsourcing projects, contributes to reducing and optimizing costs, exchanging materials, creating textbooks, conducting research, sharing knowledge and obtaining ideas for development or funding for scholarships for students, sports teams, research projects of students, academics or study trips.

With significant disruption to this educational sector this year, due to COVID-19 pandemic, the need for new delivery methods and greater collaboration has become urgent and obvious as existing structures and traditional channels have struggled to cope or have already been shut down. Crowdsourcing has significant potential to transform the education space by either enhancing existing methodologies or offering innovative possibilities to develop new pedagogical techniques. This can offer benefits for practitioners, institutions, students and participants. HEIs often fail to crowdsource successfully because crowds differ in how they are organized compared to traditional sourcing.

With the continuing increase in the use of online distributed learning environments, crowdsourcing of educational research efforts is becoming more important. Crowdsourcing is a new paradigm of educational technology development over the next few years. There are some books dealing with crowdsourcing; however, there are no publications dealing with crowdsourcing in higher education. Therefore, there is a need for practitioners and academics to further explore the innovative use of crowdsourcing in education. This book's intention is to bring together the analyses and insights of researchers and scientists worldwide, but practitioners are also more than welcomed to contribute results of their efforts. All types of contributions are considered, ranging from real-life case studies to best practices, conceptual papers, empirical studies, literature reviews, and the like. From the book you can learn what crowdsourcing in higher education is and how we can understand mechanisms (implementation and managing) of crowdsourcing in education. The possibilities of benefits and limitations of crowdsourcing in education for faculty, students, and institutions are explained. The purpose of the book is to underline the methods of adoption and managing of crowdsourcing in higher education.

This book is primarily a research monograph. The book is also the first comprehensive publication on crowdsourcing in higher education. This book provides crowdsourcing in higher education related recommendations, including functional mechanisms, different forms, applications, participant behaviours, adoption and reuse analysis, performance assessment, implementation model, critical success factors, benefits and limitations of crowdsourcing in higher education for faculty, students, and institutions (schools and higher education). Practical case studies on assessment of crowdsourcing in education are presented and that is very useful for policy makers and researchers in education, development studies, governance, public administration, sociology, innovation, school policy, school agencies, higher education, administrators and bureaucrats, policymakers and NGOs working in the area. This book shall provide readers with practical, and methodological tips how to design, development and evaluation of crowdsourcing in higher education. The solution of the research problem posed in the work required conducting literature research in order to provide a theoretical foundation. The book presents a new framework for crowdsourcing in higher education and develops valuable recommendations on how to apply it.

1 The Changing Context of Crowdsourcing in the Higher Education

Digital Transformation

Łukasz Sułkowski

1.1 Digitization, Virtualization, Digital Revolution, Digital Economy

The concept of digitization is ambiguous and various definitions can be searched for (Vial, 2019, pp. 118–144). Some of them focus on narrow understanding of digitization, such as converting data from analogue to digital (digitization), while others head towards digital transformation defined in terms of the information and communication revolution (digitalization). For the first time, this term probably appeared in the literature on the subject in 1971. Digitization of society was then perceived to be the spread of broadly understood digital and information technologies (Matt et al., 2015). Looking for a general definition, it can be indicated that digitization is a process of using information and communication tools for the effective dissemination of knowledge in the group of social actors (Reis et al., 2018).

Digitization is a technological, social and cultural process that enables rapid sharing, dissemination, interactive work and individual and team work on all kinds of data including: texts, numbers, images and sounds through the network, software and information and communication technologies. Digital technologies are differently defined in the subject literature. One of the definition methods involves enumeration of a set of technologies, which is sometimes referred to as SMACIT (Sebastian et al., 2020; Vial, 2019).

1. Social – information and communication technologies with social aspects (Brosig et al., 2020);
2. Mobile – mobile, portable and remote with the use of smartphones and mobile applications (Akoka et al., 2017);
3. Analytics – enabling the analysis of mass data (big data) allowing for making decisions based on evidence (evidence-based) (Akoka et al., 2017);
4. Cloud – the process of storing and processing data in a computing cloud (Reis et al., 2018);
5. Internet of Things (IoT) – an ecosystem of things connected with each other and exchanging data (Tambotoh et al., 2016).

DOI: 10.4324/9781003227175-2

The vast majority of these technologies are developed by means of crowdsourcing methods. In addition, digital technologies that allow for digital transformation include social networks, Internet platforms, mobile applications, utility software and blockchain (Jewitt, 2013).

It is worth asking the question about the social, cultural and organizational consequences of the broadly understood digitization processes. The first profound effect will refer to emergence of the "network society" based on new interactions involving Internet technologies that connect people through virtual ties into virtual communities. The concept of "network society" was created by J. Van Dijk in 1991 and popularized by M. Castells at the turn of the 20th and 21st centuries (Van Dijk, 1999). For Castells (2004), networks driven by digital technologies are becoming the most important nodes of social structures at all levels and gradually become the basis for the construction of individual and collective identities. In this sense, the concept of a network society is a development of the ideas of the information society and the knowledge-based economy (Castells, 2004). One of the important aspects of the development of the network society refers to the formation of the network economy. The most important resource of this economy is data, and its development engine is the strengthening of the network market based on data processing in the Internet. At the individual level, changes in the sphere of identity and shaping of interpersonal bonds are a distinct tendency (Burke, 1997). A similar process of shaping network collective identities can be observed at the organizational level (Kohtamäki et al., 2016).

Virtualization is the creation of virtual (not physical) versions of various things, using computers and information technology (Kohtamäki et al., 2016). Virtualization is about creating movies, books, photos, music and even works of art or money. Thanks to virtualization, faster, cheaper and more common access to many services is possible. What is more, entire economic sectors based on virtualization processes are now emerging, such as computer and video games, education, scientific research and technical simulations using virtual reality (VR), publishing of e-books, films and music (Rodríguez-Haro et al., 2012).

Striving to increase the efficiency and reduce the costs of an organization's operations leads to data-based decision-making systems (evidence-based decision making). Digitization contributes to improvement of intraorganizational efficiency in the area of quality, consistency and precision of the implemented processes. From a management point of view, there is greater control over organizational processes both at the operational and strategic levels. This happens thanks to an effective process of access, collection and processing of data. This is closely related to the data-based decision-making process, which has revolutionized management processes in many areas of organization and social life.

The digital revolution has its strengths and opportunities, but also potential and realized weaknesses and threats. Optimism related to the development of the network society emanates from the early ideas of the network revolution. This resembles thinking about utopian socialism by H. de Saint-Simon, Ch. Fourier and R. Owen. Such a symbolic concept emphasizing possibilities of developing open communication, democracy allowing for fuller participation of society, limiting barriers to access to knowledge and the prospects of creating open Internet communities is referred to as "network society" by M. Castells and J. Van Dijk (Van Dijk, 1999). Many hopes related to the dissemination of access to knowledge through the network have come true in recent decades. An example can be provided by Wikipedia, the open, widely available, largest encyclopaedia that overshadows French encyclopaedists and the Britannica encyclopaedia, while continuing the idea of a complete compendium of knowledge and universal access (Anthony et al., 2009). Disseminating access to scientific resources is done through evolving goggle scholar platforms and open-source projects (Ávila et al., 2018). Another example can be given by social networks that are platforms used to create network platforms. Facebook, LinkedIn, Instagram, Twitter and communication platforms including Messenger, Snapchat or WhatsApp are the basis for creating network communities that give universal, easy access to interpersonal contacts (Crews & Stitt-Gohdes, 2012; Kenchakkanavar, 2015).

Web, computer and mobile applications dominate the economic and social sphere. Computer networks also pose a number of threats. Reddy and Reinartz (2017) pay attention to negative aspects of digitization including production of huge amounts of redundant data, social changes leading to a sense of alienation and growing aspirations in digital consumption. As for the latter characteristic, "ostentatious consumption" described by T. Veblen (Bagwell & Bernheim, 1996) is an interesting phenomenon.

Do networking and digitization lead to the democratization of consumption and a departure from "ostentatious consumption"? It seems that not at all. There are completely new manifestations observed in the form of digital "for show" consumption, for example, acquisition of rights to digital works of art. Internet "for show" consumption is used to distinguish elites, structure and outline status differences (Ismail et al., 2018).

The digital revolution is leading to multi-level social, economic and cultural changes (Barnatt, 2001). Behavioural changes appear and perpetuate at the individual level. People are becoming consumers of digital goods, which most often take intangible forms. Educational services, e-commerce, computer games and movies, texts, photos and videos are increasingly used dematerialized digital products, which are replacing older technological generations of market products (Breeding, 2013). Dematerialization, virtualization and the shift towards services are other features of the digital transformation (Griffiths, 2013; Hadad & Bratianu, 2019; Van Der Merwe, 1999). Digital consumers are characterized by readiness for network cooperation and product co-creation (crowdsourcing), flexibility and sometimes even ephemeral, relationality and virtualization (Gilleard, 2017; McQuade et al., 1996; Nicholas et al., 2008).

The network economy and digital consumer are factors influencing transformation of an organization towards digitization. This transformation can be described by the following four features: virtualization, networking, agility, responsiveness and value co-creation.

Digital transformation of organizations strengthens the area of uncertainty by coupling technology with the social and cultural spheres:

1 The degree of complexity of the digital transformation exceeds the level characterizing implementation of new information and communication technologies because it triggers the feedback processes.
2 Organizational boundaries are blurring as a result of digitization and networking.
3 Physical and digital interdependence strengthens innovation processes as a result of coupling the effects of different technologies.
4 Behaviour of a digitized client is difficult to predict.

Summarizing this literature review on the digital transformation of societies, one can find common, universal features of this long-term change occurring on a global scale. Eight permanent trends can be identified when looking for the most important manifestations of the digital transformation of societies.

1 Shaping new behavioural patterns of the digital consumer, recipient and client that is focused on the perception, use and interpretation of digital goods (Zwick & Dholakia, 2004).
2 The network and information economy is developing. Importance of dematerialized products and services is growing (Moutinho & Heitor, 2007).
3 Development of the digital services and innovation market, which dynamically grow and absorb subsequent economic sectors, marginalizing the importance of older generations of products (Quattrociocchi et al., 2017).
4 The primacy of information and communication technologies in shaping social activities and in directing cultural and economic changes (Barbet & Coutinet, 2001; Moreno 2014).
5 Creation of new communities and network ties as well as new social and cultural patterns based on digital competences (Feenberg & Barney, 2004).
6 Progressive changes in organizations and organizational networks towards digitization and networking and faster absorption of information and communication technologies (Ballantyne & LaMendola, 2010).

7 Strengthening of information and communication technologies as a key field of gaining competitive advantage by organizations (Mu et al., 2010).
8 Progress in the concept of value co-creation by network communities and value co-creation with the client (Ballantyne & LaMendola, 2010; Chan et al., 2015).

1.2 Organizations of the Digital Age

Digital absorption by organizations is a process that can be judged in terms of a long-term revolution and a paradigm shift. Instead of entrenched solutions building a competitive position on the basis of the composition of natural and human resources, access to knowledge resources and competences related to their processing and dissemination begin to play a dominant role. Digital technologies additionally require an effective management process of these unique resources at the level of the entire organization (Uzzi, 1996). Adaptation of digital technologies is an organizational, social and cultural process driving change in general (Castells, 2000).

People and organizations are under pressure from the rapid development of information and communication technologies as a result of technological advances and the development of competition in most sectors (Innes & Booher, 1999). This has consequences in the form of development of the risk society, increased uncertainty in activity, blurring of organizational boundaries and changes in economic and socio-cultural systems. Comprehensively, these changes are closely related to networking, digitization, automation and robotization (Caruso, 2018). Many researchers point to several possible manifestations of the development of new forms of digital organization related to the development of information and communication technologies, including: cloud computing services (Akande et al., 2013), IoT, Internet of Everything (Samaniego & Deters, 2016; Yao et al., 2015), hyperconnectivity (Fredette et al., 2012), software model understood as a service (Software-as-a-Service – Saas) (Agarwal, 2011) and big data analytics (BDA) (Choi et al., 2018). The revolutionary changes taking place on the basis of information and communication technologies are captured in a diverse cognitive framework (Afonasova et al., 2019). Examples of alliances of management concepts with IT ideas may be found in the following approaches: agile, reengineering, NBIC and many others (Yu & Mylopoulus, 1996). Agile is an organizational and IT solution for the production of high-quality software. The principles of the "Agile Manifesto", which combines IT concepts and organization and management, can be summarized by means of ten postulates:

1 achieving customer satisfaction through the speed of software development
2 working software is provided periodically (weekly rather than monthly)

3 working software is the basic measure of progress
4 late changes in the specification do not have a destructive effect on the software development process
5 close, daily cooperation between the business and the developer
6 direct contact as the best form of communication within and outside the team;
7 constant attention focused on technical aspects and good design
8 simplicity
9 self-management of teams
10 regular adaptation to changing requirements (Krehbiel et al., 2017)

Reengineering (business process re-engineering) is a management concept developed in the 1990s, based on the assumption of a radical restructuring of organizational processes resulting from computerization processes (Hammer & Champy, 2009). In computer science, reengineering can be equated with code refactoring, i.e., restructuring an existing programme without changing its function and operation. NBIC (nano-bio-info-cogno) (Stępień, 2015) technologies is a set of a system of practical solutions and conceptualization as well as the ability to apply them (know-how) as well as methods, procedures and technologies that use this knowledge (Kolbachev & Kolbacheva, 2018; Volkova et al., 2017).

Analysing the directions of development of the organization of the digital age, several tendencies that stem from absorption of information and communication technologies by people in socio-cultural systems can be discussed. Organization virtualization refers to application of virtual methods and tools in an organization and management (Verdouw et al., 2015). Agile organization is, in turn, a method of managing creation and implementation of IT projects (Gandomani & Nafchi, 2016; Rigby et al., 2016). Another example of the expansion of digital management methods may be provided by co-creation of value by network communities (crowdsourcing and crowdfunding) (Siala, 2013). From the point of view of organization management, the collection and processing of mass data (BDA; McAfee et al., 2012) and making decisions based on data (evidence-based decision making) are also important.

Organizations use digital transformation for a variety of purposes. The first differentiation indicates information and communication technologies that are a digital product or a process supporting their functioning (Schmitt, 2018). Transforming an organization under the influence of digital change may lead to cost reduction, as well as increasing quality, efficiency and effectiveness (Casalino et al., 2021), developing communication with customers and the environment or acquiring digital consumers (Berman, 2012; Nicholas & Rowlands, 2008). The digital transformation of an organization can therefore go in various directions: strategy, technology, values, structure and finances (Adner et al., 2019; Matt et al., 2015). Development and implementation of new information and communication technologies are accompanied by various management concepts. The historical ones include reengineering. The ones gaining in importance refer to: Industry 4.0, Industrial Revolution 4.0 IoT, SMART (Shao et al., 2021; Shrouf et al., 2014).

Information and communication technologies used as the basis of management processes include the following processes: computerization, digitization, robotization (cyber-physical systems), VR, processing and analysis of mass data in real time (BDA), IoT ecosystem (Internet of Services), inter-organizational relations, co-opetition (strategic partnering, knowledge partnering and co-opetition), artificial intelligence, neural networks, fuzzy logic and soft computing, machine learning and machine to machine communications.

The market role of information and communication technologies relates to shaping relationships with customers and stakeholders, managing the strategic and operational activities of the organization in the area of providing services to the market (Lu et al., 2013; Zhang et al., 2011), providing new or enriched values for customers (Kucia et al., 2021; Pynnönen et al., 2011), shaping business by means of digital perspectives, creating opportunities for co-creating value with customers (Breidbach & Maglio, 2016; Heim et al., 2018).

The digital transformation of an organization is related to the strategic and operational aspects. The scale of digital transformation in the enterprise leads to strategic changes and to a fundamental reconstruction of strategic and operational processes. This, in turn, leads, in the case of the economic activity, to creation and implementation of new business models. Digital technologies are implemented in organizations most often through operational spheres, which also affect the strategy:

1 technical infrastructure (hardware, equipment),
2 application, utility and organizational software (software),
3 system and communication infrastructure,
4 integration of business processes with external contractors.

Organizational strategy is often closely related to digital transformation (Sebastian et al., 2020). First of all, it may refer to development of the organization resulting from the emergence of a new digital market that was not there before. This happens in the case of the enterprises that deal with the following: computer hardware and software, implementation of solutions in the field of information and communication technologies, e-commerce, social media, the IoT or crowdsourcing (Kim et al., 2008). Development of entire sectors initially takes the form of a blue ocean strategy, in which enterprises become market and technology leaders that are gradually followed by others (Pillania & Chang, 2009). Obvious examples of such entities are "Behemoths", called "gafas" because of their quasi-monopolistic or oligopolistic market power, i.e., Google, Apple,

Facebook and Amazon. Manufacturing and implementation companies are directly related to the software and hardware sector, where, for example, Microsoft and IBM can be considered market leaders. The strategic aspect can also relate to the fundamental reconstruction of the core business and its enrichment with completely new functions (Correani et al., 2020; Gobble, 2018; Kane et al., 2015; Matt et al., 2015). A good example is given by the market reconstruction of the activities undertaken by many companies producing mobile phones, stemming from the technological revolution related to the emergence and popularization of smartphones.

Development of the Industry and Society 4.0 concept, which has been taking place since 2011, also leads to a change in business models from product orientation to service orientation (Gajdzik & Grabowska, 2018). Business models are based on the integration and cooperation of entities in providing services to customers. Collaboration of humans with digital machines creates market value, enables flexibility and drives the innovation process on the IoT and the Internet of People. This open communication between people and digital machines on the Internet results in information transparency allowing for the improvement of services (interconnectivity and information transparency). Decentralized decisions based on continuous communication and data analysis allow flexibility in production and management. Network methods of organization and management as well as digital tools play a key role in this trend (Almada-Lobo, 2015; Lasi et al., 2014; Morrar et al., 2017).

The digitization of large sectors of society is changing practices in business, but also in social services, education, health, social care, journalism, entertainment and so on (Larsson & Teigland, 2019; Saxena, 2021). Higher education is not immune to these changes. Digitization processes are already underway and the potential for new opportunities is significant. In the literature on the subject, it is possible to find many different aspects of managing organizations in digital transformation. Examples include several approaches and models: "cybernetic", "technological", "value creation", "structural change", and "finance" (Matt et al., 2015). "Cybernetic" organization management model describes a process whose input is data acquisition, and then transformation (algorithmic or heuristic) towards information, and the process itself is closed by knowledge diffusion. Digital transformation can be based on the selection of priorities related to technology, value creation, change or finance. The use of technology refers to a company's attitude to new technologies as well as its ability to use these technologies. The role of ICT (Information and Communication Technologies) is fundamental to the company's operations as it is the product core on which the company's strategy is built. This is related to deciding what market position the entity is striving for: a technological leader or a follower. Being a technological leader in the market may lead to a competitive advantage, but it also involves uncertainty and risk, because the technology that is to be the core of the business may not yet be developed and its possibilities are unknown. From a business point of view, the use of new technologies often means changes in value creation. They concern the impact of the digital transformation strategy on the "value" of online companies, i.e., how far new digital activities differ from classic, often still basic business. The changes create opportunities to expand and enrich the current portfolio of products and services, and to transform the business model into one that shall be more suited to the changing market. Digitization of products or services may enable or require various forms of profit generation (monetization), and even the adjustment of the business scope of the strategy, if the products are targeted at other markets or at new customer segments. Structural changes often go hand in hand with different technologies to provide an appropriate basis for new operations. Structural changes relate to changes in a company's configuration, especially with regard to placement of a new digital activity within corporate structures. Therefore, it is important to assess the scale of changes resulting from the digital transformation of the enterprise. If the scope of the changes is fairly limited, it may make more sense to integrate the new operations into existing corporate structures, while for more significant changes it would be better to create a separate subsidiary within the company. The financial aspect leads to an assessment of what financing models will result from the digital transformation in the enterprise.

1.3 The Digital Transformation of Higher Education

The literature review on the subject indicates several ways of understanding the digital transformation of universities (Benavides et al., 2020; Simonette et al., 2021). Organizing these definitions and areas, several leading threads can be seen including change management, digital breakthrough, educational innovation, customer adaptation and new business models (Hess et al., 2016; Matt et al., 2015; Vial, 2019).

1. Digital transformation (DT) is a process of changes in the university and includes people, processes, strategies and structures understood dynamically (Rodrigues, 2017; Wade, 2021). TC is "a process that aims to change the organization as a whole through a combination of information, computing, communication and connectivity technologies" (Vial, 2019). The organization aims to control TC, which takes place in the planned change management process (Tabrizi et al., 2019).
2. Digital disruption is defined as changes caused or catalysed by digital technologies that disrupt established ways of creating value, social interaction, doing business and our thinking in general (Sullivan & Staib, 2018). The concept of digital breakthrough is closely related to digital transformation and disruptive innovations (Lim, 2019). The implementation of digital technologies in many types of business activity, but also in many aspects of social life, leads to a rapid change

in the way we operate. We are dealing with such a digital breakthrough during a pandemic, when the activity of universities moved to the virtual world (Telli & Aydin, 2021).

3 DT can be understood as adaptation or new investments in technologies and business models in order to engage customers more effectively at every stage of the life cycle (Berman, 2012; Puriwat & Tripopsakul, 2021).

4 Companies have had to think of digital transformation as "formal efforts to renew business vision, models and investments towards a new digital economy" (Betchoo, 2016; Zhao et al., 2020).

5 This is DT's strategic and marketing perspective. The new strategy using DT should include commitment and co-creating market value with customers (Malar et al., 2019; Mihardjo et al., 2019).

6 Digital transformation goes far beyond dematerialization of processes, including the innovative use of new technologies to promote new services, redefine business models and interact with users (Faria & Nóvoa, 2020). DT is the process of creating and implementing innovations that change the market and organizations leading to new solutions (Hinings et al., 2018; Nambisan et al., 2019).

7 The digital transformation of the higher education system should be of wider interest and must include modernization of IT architecture management, which could significantly contribute to innovation in education. There has been a rapid increase in the number of research on TC in higher education in recent years. There is a growing interest in the implementation of ICT solutions in the activities of universities, which is aimed at a digital university (Bond et al., 2018). In the Google Scholar search engine, under the index: "digital transformation" + "higher education", there were 21,300 entries, of which as many as 17,000 came from the last three years (downloaded: August 8, 2021).

8 An important topic at DT of the university refers to modern solutions used to modernize the educational system with the help of ICT technology and the integration of digital technologies in teaching, learning and organizational practices (Fleaca, 2011). The problems of education with the use of digital methods and tools lie at the junction of the university's second mission and digital transformation. Frequently used topics include e-learning didactics, the use of information and communication solutions in education, the analysis of digital interaction and communication in the teaching process (Androutsos & Brinia, 2019; Bonfiglio-Pavisich, 2018; Lorenzo & Gallon, 2019; Zain, 2021).

9 Digital transformation is accelerated evolution. It is also a revolution due to its radical and structural implications for people and infrastructure, which also require new educational and business models (Gama, 2018). New business models and management methods often require fundamental rethinking and designing the following key issues: strategy, product, customer and target market (Tabrizi et al., 2019).

10 Digital transformation can be defined as the modification of business processes, opportunities and policies in order to take advantage of the changes and opportunities created by new technologies, as well as their impact on society (Sandhu, 2018). From the management point of view, the importance of DT's influence on business processes is increasing, but also on public organizations, non-profit activities and public policies. Originally, the largest number of research and implementation took place in business, but as DT progresses, the share of public and non-commercial sectors increases (Curtis, 2019; Kokkinakos et al., 2016; Mergel et al., 2018).

Summarizing the presented ways of interpreting the meaning of digital transformation in higher education, it is worth pointing to a few common elements found in the literature on the subject. First of all, TC is treated as a breakthrough process, leading to profound changes in many aspects of the university's operations. The multidimensionality of changes caused by TC covers the following aspects: organization and management, pedagogy, infrastructure, academic culture and technology. As a result, the university generates new organization, management, teaching, research and implementation. Organizational dimensions within universities, which are often radically transformed under the influence of TC, also include strategy and management: knowledge, human capital, marketing, finances, processes and projects. Digital transformation research in higher education follows an inductive and analytical approach. There is a lack of a synthetic theoretical view based on the research results that would allow us to understand the ongoing change (Benavides et al., 2020).

1.4 Management of Digital University

The University of the Fourth Wave or Generation is a new formation in which a transformation will take place, subordinated to the logic of global changes aimed at networking and digitization of societies and people (Strielkowski & Wang, 2020). We have been dealing with pioneering solutions developing the digital organization of universities since the beginning of the 21st century, but the catalyst for changes that will accelerate the crystallization of this formation may be attributed to the COVID-19 pandemic, which in 2020/2021 made universities switch to remote activities both in the field of university management and in the case of didactics, research and implementation of the third mission (Ahrens & Zascerinska, 2020; Kulikowski et al., 2021; Rohman et al., 2020; Velásquez & Lara, 2021).

It is likely that the changes in the organization, culture and mentality will prove to be permanent and will contribute to development of digital universities (Davey and Galan-Muros, 2020; Johnston et al., 2018a; Sangster et al., 2020). This formation arises primarily as a result of the transformation of entrepreneurial universities in the 21st century, most often carried out as a planned, strategic change and project management process, which is driven by digital transformation being a civilization change (Gehrke, 2014; McCluskey & Winter, 2012). The fundamental values of the fourth wave universities include scientific and educational network, knowledge management, competitiveness, countability and open science. The values are based on digital transformation leading to the development of intelligent digital organizations, the activities of which are based on network activities based on implemented information and communication technologies (abbreviation: ICT) (Hazemi et al., 2012; McCluskey & Winter, 2012).

The transformation of science and didactics is leading to creation of a research network of virtual research teams that will connect scientists but will also be open to practitioners on the international scale. The basis for the development of such teams will be provided by research networks created through scientific social media (e.g., Research Gate and Kudos). Similarly, in the area of didactics, forms of work and communication with students will be developed by means of e-learning systems (LMS class), communicators (e.g., Zoom, MS Teams and Google Meet) and network software in the cloud. IT will become the dominant disciplinary discourse on which the logic of the functioning of digital universities is based (Khalid et al., 2018; Pacholak, 2020). In addition, the logic of management sciences will be significant at all times, with a focus on knowledge management and competitiveness. The knowledge management methodology leading to the development of a network intelligent organization uses synergy with ICT (Jones, 2013). The activities of universities will increasingly move to the Internet, where research (Hassan, 2017) and didactics (Losh, 2014), cooperation with the environment (Lundberg & Öberg, 2021), people management (Johnston et al., 2018), marketing and finance (Peters & Jandrić, 2018) would be a prerequisite for organization development and competitiveness. The alliance of IT and management in activities undertaken by universities leads to the concept of evidence-based management, which is the basis for accountability (Selwyn et al., 2018). The basis for the development of countability are ICT including big data analysis, cloud computing, crowdsourcing (Mitchell, 2002), IoT, mass on-line courses (Selwyn et al., 2018), specialized educational and organizational software (LMS, SIS, ERP) (Mosteanu, 2020a). The digital transformation of universities is based on disruptive information and communication technologies that relatively quickly transform, sometimes radically, the practice of education (Arnold et al., 2010; Bell & Cain, 2017; MacNeill et al., 2015), conducting research and implementation (Rakonjac & Jednak, 2012) and university management (Gehrke, 2014; Johnston et al., 2018; Smyth et al., 2015) and creating an IT infrastructure for virtual campuses (Mosteanu, 2020a, 2020b). Competitiveness and accountability will favour the creation of organizational systems based on knowledge, information and data management, which will control the functioning of universities more and more effectively. Development of measures of the effectiveness of scientific, educational and implementation activities will allow construction of systems for the evaluation and motivation of employees monitoring work efficiency (Canhoto et al., 2016). The spread of remote education and work as well as the globalization of science will probably lead to fiercer competition in the higher education sector, where universities will compete for students' scientific achievements and their implementation on an international scale.

The development of countability coupled with evidence-based management will also be of key importance in scientific activity. Professionalization of human capital management leads to "quasi-corporate" systems of evaluation and motivation of academics, based on the analysis of mass data on scientific achievements compared on a global scale using scientometry (Raffaghelli et al., 2016). The deepening of academic crowdsourcing, international cooperation in a network based not only on scientific communication, but also on the co-creation of value, will strengthen the open science approach, which is dominated by universal and free access to publications and results of scientific research on the Internet (Peters & Jandrić, 2018; Sitnicki, 2018). The value of such an approach is not only the democratization of science and popularization of access to knowledge, as well as facilitating and reducing the costs of research and higher education, but also more effective verification of research results and their replication (Munafò et al., 2017). Open science is about universal and free access to publications, but also information, data, research results and application software for scientific purposes.

The term "open science" was created in 1998 and quickly spread, leading to establishing and opening access to many scientific journals and publications, to the organization of open repositories and archives at universities, to legislative activities supporting the dissemination of access, to the organization of conferences and to issuing reports and declarations developing open science (2003 Berlin Declaration, 2007 OECD Report and 2019 UNESCO Conference) (González, 2005; Vicente-Saez & Martinez-Fuentes, 2018). Based on the growing scale and scope of open science, it is likely that it will be one of the values of a digital university. Thanks to universal, free access to research results, it will be faster and more effective to verify, disseminate, organize and even finance research (e.g., crowdfunding) (Fecher & Friesike, 2014).

Scientific activity undertaken at a digital university will be part of the organizational and management processes carried out on the basis of an integrated information and communication system at universities that provides reliable information. The science using the concepts and methods of knowledge management will be based on strategic, process and project management, coupled with human capital and talent management. Likewise, the educational activity and the third mission of the digital university will be managed and accounted for by an ICT system providing information for evidence-based decision making. Education will use quality systems and measures of effectiveness and satisfaction with education. Hybridization of education combining e-learning with contact forms and based on significant technological support is a possible scenario.

The third mission will remain very important, especially for the involved universities, and will probably be programmed and integrated with the counting system as well. Similarly, technology transfer, protection of intellectual rights and patents (Raffaghelli et al., 2016) will be more and more advanced and based on ICT. Authority in the university takes managerial and team forms, which is a change in relation to the third-generation universities, in which there was a decreasing scope of collective power. As a business model, management and project teams will participate in the management and supervision of the university, most often leaving decisions and responsibility with academic managers. The strategy will take the form of mission, goals, plans and strategic analysis as well as strategic management based on controlling. Controlling will be an organizational process serving to quantify the achievement of scientific, didactic, implementation and other goals. The basis for its implementation will be an integrated ICT system that processes and analyses data serving managerial decisions at all levels (data-driven decision making; Hazemi & Hailes, 2001). Organizational structures will evolve towards network and multidimensional (tensor) solutions, which is related to the flexibility of the organization. At the same time, it is likely to maintain a strong centre with departments and administrative units moving towards increased specialization. The organization will take a virtual form through the full participation of employees in the ICT system in a different nature depending on the scope of duties (managerial decisions, quality of education, scientific achievements, project management, etc.) (Bajunid, 2004). A digital university will be a learning network organization; centralized and specialized, and on the other hand, flexible and managerial.

The university staff will specialize, depending on the university's mission, in the following roles: scientific, research and teaching, education or cooperation with the academic environment. The flexibility of universities in the forms of cooperation and employment of employees will be similarly significant (Sheail, 2018; Svensson et al., 2019). Of course, it will be possible to flexibly combine organizational roles, but due to the settlement of work results, it is likely that specialization will be rewarded. An effective researcher is not necessarily a good educator, and vice versa. The roles of managers and administrative staff will be permanent and highly specialized (Mitchell, 2002). The level of complexity in managing a digital university increases as the analysis of large amounts of data should reduce the uncertainty resulting from operating in a turbulent and competitive environment (Maltese, 2018). Change management will be a permanent process and will be carried out on the basis of data that will be used to make managerial decisions (Selwyn et al., 2018). Professionalization of management will be related to specialization of administration, university staff, implementation of ICT systems supporting all processes at the university, the development of functional areas of management (human capital management, marketing, information management and finance). The administration of the university will be expanded both within the existing areas and adding new ones (e.g., the information department and the Chief Information Officer). Administrative employees who do not belong to the university's research and teaching staff will be able to perform managerial functions. Financing of universities will be diversified and based on many sources: public and private funds, student tuition fees, research grants, income from cooperation with business and the environment. A further reduction in the state funding is likely, combined with a tendency to increase the importance of funding for effects and goals in accountability systems (Brown, 2018; Mosteanu, 2020a).

The supervision of HEIs will remain differentiated according to the type of HEI and the national system. Although in general it seems that in this area there will be international governance convergence of higher education. The general tendency is the evolution towards fairly general regulations for universities and setting goals and financial incentive systems for universities that achieve their goals and the best scientific and didactic results. This leaves a lot of autonomy to public universities in the selection of methods of achieving results. Non-public universities, which usually have less funding from state budgets, will be subject to even weaker regulations related mainly to accreditations and more and more detailed reporting (Aitchison et al., 2020). As in the case of any entrepreneurial university, academic freedom will be limited by finances, the university's own strategy and public politicians, as well as practical orientation in the field of the third mission. Non-priority research for universities and non-profit-generating research will not be developed (McCluskey & Winter, 2014).

The formation of a digital university leads to effective intelligent organizations improving in the creation, management and transfer of knowledge. Data-based decision-making, constantly optimized processes, strategy and structure, developed ICT and accountability systems as well as advanced management methods indicate a high level of professionalization in the implementation of the academic mission. However, this potential organizational excellence has its dangers. The pendulum is tilting, moving farther and farther away from the Universities of the Second Wave and academic freedom towards the Universities of the Fourth Wave, in which the core role is played by power and control (Hassan, 2017; Lacković, 2020). This involves some danger voiced by critics of the neoliberal entrepreneurial university (Laalo et al., 2019; Liesner, 2006; Rhoads, 2018). A digital university poses an additional threat of a digital panopticon, consisting in the perfect control of knowledge workers (Johnston et al., 2018).

This threatens with alienation (Hopkins, 2015), the dissolution of professional ties, the commercialization and corporatization of the world of universities, and a complete erosion of ethos and academic culture (Johnston et al., 2018). An attempt to counteract the falling from the utopia of academic freedom of a Humboldt-type university into a dystopia of power and managerial control of a digital university may be reflection, critical thinking and a discussion about the conditions for creating committed digital universities (MacNeill et al., 2020; Peters et al., 2020).

The perspective of the centuries-long transformation of universities from the perspective of the discourse of organization and management presented in this chapter leads to several conclusions resulting from the comparison of successive waves of universities (Table 1.1).

Firstly, the fundamental mission of universities remains unchanged in essence, although strategic diversification leads to different types of universities that focus on selected aspects of the mission in their activities. Examples include research universities, applied sciences universities, professional colleges and corporate colleges. This means that universities have not lost their organizational identity and, despite dynamic changes, knowledge organizations remain focused on science, education and relations with the environment. A significant change concerns the design and implementation of the university's diversified missions. The field of study ranges from a uniform understanding of the role of universities in waves I and II, to the diversification of missions and strategies in waves III and IV. For traditional universities, the mission that is socially accepted, reflected in academic culture and internalized by staff and students is learning coupled with education. For waves III and IV universities, the mission is its own construct of identity and organizational culture, which takes into account three social roles, but adapts the mission to the specificity of the academic institution.

Secondly, the role of the academic culture and ethos, which was the most important bond of the organization for the universities of the first and second waves, is changing. Initially, the integration of employees and students took place thanks to entering a specific circle of values, norms, rituals and cultural patterns. Despite the many changes and diversity of universities, tradition regulated people's behaviour, gave them identity and determined the ways of organization, management and exercise of power.

Along with the development of the third wave of universities in the 20th century, the rigid academic culture is transforming into a culture of entrepreneurship drawing its models from business. At the same time, there is some expansion of concepts and management methods that radically change functioning of universities, previously based on academic culture and ethos. Professionalization of university management contributes to the increase in the efficiency of their operation, but at the same time creates resistance to bureaucratization, commercialization, managerism and corporatization of the academic world (Laalo et al., 2019; Peters, 2012).

Table 1.1 Four waves of universities – a comparative analysis

Criterion	University of the first wave *Medieval and enlightenment*	University of the second wave *Humboldt*	University of the third wave *Enterprising, post-Humboldt*	University of the fourth wave *Digital*
Rise and reform	Spontaneous or assumed by rulers	A university or reform plan based on the Humboldt project	Strategic plan and project management of changes	Strategy, project management and controlling
Chronology	11th–18th century	19th century–mid 20th century	1970–present	21st century
Values	Teaching students by masters	Building, cultural and nation-building ideas integrating the nation and the state	Competition, market, academic entrepreneurship	Scientific and educational network, knowledge management, competitiveness, countability, open science
Formation	Elite	Elite	Egalitarian	Egalitarian
Academic culture	Community of baccalaureates and students	The elite of professors (masters) and students	Competitive, flexible organization of knowledge	Network organization of knowledge
Dominant discourse	Various, theology, philosophy, law	Philosophy and humanities	Management sciences, economics	Computer science, management sciences
Authority	Collective guild	Collective academic community	Managerial and collective	Managerial and team
Missions	Education and research, uniform	Education related to science and culture, uniform	Science, education and the third mission, diversified	Specialization: science, education and third mission
Strategy	Traditional goals, spontaneous development	Ethical goals, set directions of development	Emergent strategy or strategic plan, mission and formulated goals	Strategy – plan, mission, evidence-based goals, controlling
Structure	Traditional, rigid cells	Traditional, hierarchical, fixed	Matrix, with a strong decision-making centre, a growing level of specialization	Networked, with a strong decision-making centre, flexible, specialized

(Continued)

Table 1.1 Four waves of universities – a comparative analysis (Continued)

Criterion	University of the first wave — Medieval and enlightenment	University of the second wave — Humboldt	University of the third wave — Enterprising, post-Humboldt	University of the fourth wave — Digital
Organization of the university	Hierarchical, stable, academic	Loose, bureaucratic, decentralized, stable, academic	Strict – headquarters, loose – the periphery, flexible, elements of centralization and decentralization, managerial and academic	Networked, flexible, centralized, managerial
People	Traditional roles and responsibilities	Traditional roles and responsibilities	Flexible, variable roles of staff, specialized and permanent administration	Flexible, variable roles and permanent administration, specialization
Management	Minimized, regulated by tradition	Limited, planned in the project, ethos	Extensive, planned and entrepreneurial, professionalization	Extensive, analytical, planned, based on data and evidence, professionalization
Administration	Very limited, managed by an elected academic staff	Very limited, managed by an elected academic staff	Expanded and growing, specialized managerial functions	Expanded and growing, specialized managerial functions
Financing	Various, private, state, church	Public, state-owned, both for research and teaching missions	Various, public – state, private – external founders	Various, often mixed, public universities, more often state-owned
Supervision	Limited, internal	None, internal, academic	Various, often mixed, public universities, more often state-owned	Big, general, external
University autonomy	Large, varied models	Very large, varied models	Large, varied models	Large, varied models
Academic freedom	Big in relation to society, limited by hierarchical culture	Very large, freedom in the selection of research issues and methods, students and colleagues	Moderate, limited by finances and practical orientation	Moderate, limited by finances, strategy and politics as well as practical orientation

Source: Own study.

The critical trend in management and radical positions (gender studies, neo-Marxism and postmodernism) reject the neoliberal transformation of universities arising from the discourse of contemporary turbo-capitalism. The domination of instrumental reason in the form of placing on the pedestal of efficiency, competition and the market may lead universities to depart from focusing on the civilization mission: reaching the truth and proclaiming it and transforming them into knowledge corporations producing symbolic private goods (Alajoutsijärvi et al., 2013; Berglund et al., 2020; Hurd & Singh, 2020). Digital universities may carry similar threats, magnified by the culture of control developing, thanks to the digital panopticon (Strielkowski & Wang, 2020).

Thirdly, the organizational characteristics of universities in the 21st century combine the development of information and communication technologies with implementation of management concepts and methods. Progressive networking, digitization and computerization of universities are persistent trends that have been intertwined with management through accountability and data-based decision-making, as well as an audit and control culture. Despite the resistance of part of the academic community and students, progress in the development of digitization in universities is likely, because the drive will be an increase in efficiency in achieving goals.

Fourthly, the degree of advancement of universities in the application of management concepts, methods and techniques increases. Based on business models, concepts of new public management and public value management, universities professionalize further aspects of their activities: finance and accounting, marketing, human capital management, processes, projects, knowledge and information. The consequence is an increase in control and managerial power, but at the same time a potential danger of university bureaucratization.

To sum up, we need some critical reflection and the development of the concept of participatory management of a digital university, which will allow to organize universities so that they could maintain their identity and would not lose their academic values and civilization mission, thus achieving some balance between the utopia of academic freedom and the dystopia of managerial power and control. This journey between Scylla and Charybdis requires the involvement of the academic community and university stakeholders in a dialogue that allows for the development of compromise solutions (Sulkowski, 2022).

References

Adner, R., Puranam, P., & Zhu, F. (2019). What is different about digital strategy? From quantitative to qualitative change. *Strategy Science*, 4(4), 253–261.

Agarwal, P. (2011). Continuous SCRUM: Agile management of SAAS products [Conference session]. *Proceedings of the 4th India Software Engineering Conference* (pp. 51–60), Thiruvananthapuram, India.

Ahrens, A., & Zascerinska, J. (2020). Post-COVID-19 university governance in Germany. *Education Reform: Education Content Research and Implementation Problems, 2*, 7–16.

Aitchison, C., Harper, R., Mirriahi, N., & Guerin, C. (2020). Tensions for educational developers in the digital university: Developing the person, developing the product. *Higher Education Research & Development, 39*(2), 171–184.

Akande, A. O., April, N. A., & Van Belle, J. P. (2013). Management issues with cloud computing [Conference session]. *Proceedings of the Second International Conference on Innovative Computing and Cloud Computing* (pp. 119–124), Wuhan, China.

Akoka, J., Comyn-Wattiau, I., & Laoufi, N. (2017). Research on big data—A systematic mapping study. *Computer Standards & Interfaces, 54*, 105–115.

Alajoutsijärvi, K., Juusola, K., & Siltaoja, M. (2013). Academic capitalism hits the fan: The birth of acamanic capitalism. *Getting things done*. Emerald Group Publishing Limited.

Almada-Lobo, F. (2015). The industry 4.0 revolution and the future of manufacturing execution systems (MES). *Journal of Innovation Management, 3*(4), 16–21.

Androutsos, A., & Brinia, V. (2019). Developing and piloting a pedagogy for teaching innovation, collaboration, and co-creation in secondary education based on design thinking, digital transformation, and entrepreneurship. *Education Sciences, 9*(2), 113.

Anthony, D., Smith, S. W., & Williamson, T. (2009). Reputation and reliability in collective goods: The case of the online encyclopedia Wikipedia. *Rationality and Society, 21*(3), 283–306.

Arnold, K. E., Tanes, Z., & King, A. S. (2010). Administrative perceptions of data-mining software signals: Promoting student success and retention. *The Journal of Academic Administration in Higher Education, 6*(2), 29–39.

Ávila, L., Teixeira, L., & Almeida, P. (2018). A methodological approach to dematerialization of business processes using open-source technology. *International Journal of Industrial Engineering and Management, 9*(3), 121–128.

Bagwell, L. S., & Bernheim, B. D. (1996). Veblen effects in a theory of conspicuous consumption. *The American Economic Review*, 349–373.

Bajunid, I. A. (2004). Preliminary explorations of knowledge management initiative in higher educational institution: The case of the quality management major/concentration undergraduate degree program in a virtual university. *Malaysian Journal of Learning & Instruction, 1*(1), 1–29.

Ballantyne, N., & LaMendola, W. (2010). Human services in the network society: Introduction to the special issue. *Journal of Technology in Human Services, 28*(1–2), 1–6.

Barbet, P., & Coutinet, N. (2001). Measuring the digital economy: State-of-the-art developments and future prospects. *Communications and Strategies, 42*(2), 153–184.

Barnatt, C. (2001). The second digital revolution. *Journal of General Management, 27*(2), 1–16.

Bell, J., & Cain, W. (2017). Online education policy and practice: The past, present, and future of the digital university. *Teachers College Record*.

Benavides, L. M. C., Tamayo Arias, J. A., Arango Serna, M. D., Branch Bedoya, J. W., & Burgos, D. (2020). Digital transformation in higher education institutions: A systematic literature review. *Sensors, 20*(11), 3291.

Berglund, K., Hytti, U., & Verduijn, K. (2020). Navigating the terrain of entrepreneurship education in neoliberal societies. *Entrepreneurship Education and Pedagogy, 4*(4), 702–717.

Berman, S. J. (2012). Digital transformation: Opportunities to create new business models, *Strategy & Leadership, 40*(2), 16–24.

Betchoo, N. K. (2016, August 3–6). Digital transformation and its impact on human resource management: A case analysis of two unrelated businesses in the Mauritian public service [Conference session]. *Proceedings of the 2016 IEEE International Conference on Emerging Technologies and Innovative Business Practices for the Transformation of Societies (EmergiTech)*, Balaclava, Mauritius.

Bond, M., Marín, V. I., Dolch, C., Bedenlier, S., & Zawacki-Richter, O. (2018). Digital transformation in German higher education: Student and teacher perceptions and usage of digital media. *International Journal of Educational Technology in Higher Education, 15*(1), 1–20.

Bonfiglio-Pavisich, N. (2018). Technology and pedagogy integration: A model for meaningful technology integration. *Australian Educational Computing, 33*(1).

Bowersox, D. J., Closs, D. J., & Drayer, R. W. (2005). The digital transformation: Technology and beyond. *Supply Chain Management Review, 9*(1), 22–29.

Breeding, M. (2013, September). Cloud computing: A new generation of technology enables deeper collaboration. In *International symposium on information management in a changing world* (pp. 25–35). Springer.

Breidbach, C. F., & Maglio, P. P. (2016). Technology-enabled value co-creation: An empirical analysis of actors, resources, and practices. *Industrial Marketing Management, 56*, 73–85.

Brosig, C., Westner, M., & Strahringer, S. (2020, June). Revisiting the concept of IT capabilities in the era of digitalization. *2020 IEEE 22nd Conference on Business Informatics (CBI)* (Vol. 1, pp. 84–93).

Brown, G. (2018). *Online education policy and practice: The past, present, and the future of the digital university.* Teachers College Record.

Burke, P. J. (1997). An identity model for network exchange. *American Sociological Review, 62*(1), 134–150.

Canhoto, A. I., Quinton, S., Jackson, P., & Dibb, S. (2016). The co-production of value in digital, university–industry R&D collaborative projects. *Industrial Marketing Management, 56*, 86–96.

Caruso, L. (2018). Digital innovation and the fourth industrial revolution: Epochal social changes? *Ai & Society, 33*(3), 379–392.

Casalino, N., Armenia, S., & Di Nauta, P. (2021). Inspiring the organizational change and accelerating the digital transition in public sector by systems thinking and system dynamics approaches. In *Smart education and e-learning 2021* (pp. 197–214). Springer.

Castells, M. (2000). Toward a sociology of the network society. *Contemporary Sociology, 29*(5), 693–699.

Castells, M. (2004). *The network society a cross-cultural perspective*. Edward Elgar.

Chan, K. W., Li, S. Y., & Zhu, J. J. (2015). Fostering customer ideation in crowdsourcing community: The role of peer-to-peer and peer-to-firm interactions. *Journal of Interactive Marketing, 31*, 42–62.

Choi, T. M., Wallace, S. W., & Wang, Y. (2018). Big data analytics in operations management. *Production and Operations Management, 27*(10), 1868–1883.

Correani, A., De Massis, A., Frattini, F., Petruzzelli, A. M., & Natalicchio, A. (2020). Implementing a digital strategy: Learning from the experience of three digital transformation projects. *California Management Review, 62*(4), 37–56.

Crews, T. B., & Stitt-Gohdes, W. L. (2012). Incorporating Facebook and Twitter in a service-learning project in a business communication course. *Business Communication Quarterly, 75*(1), 76–79.

Curtis, S. (2019). Digital transformation - the silver bullet to public service improvement? *Public Money & Management, 39*(5), 322–324.

Faria, J. A., & Nóvoa, H. (2020, February 5–7). Digital transformation at the University of Porto. *Proceedings of the International Conference on Exploring Services Science*, Porto, Portugal.

Fecher, B., & Friesike, S. (2014). Open science: One term, five schools of thought. In S. Bartling, & S. Friesike (Eds.), *Opening science: The evolving guide on how the internet is changing research, collaboration and scholarly publishing* (pp. 17–47). Springer.

Feenberg, A., & Barney, D. (Eds.). (2004). *Community in the digital age: Philosophy and practice*. Rowman & Littlefield Publishers.

Fleaca, E. (2011, June 20–25). Embedding digital teaching and learning practices in the modernization of higher education institutions. *Proceedings of the SGEM2017 International Multidisciplinary Scientific GeoConference*, Albena, Bulgaria.

Fredette, J., Marom, R., Steiner, K., & Witters, L. (2012). The promise and peril of hyperconnectivity for organizations and societies. The Global Information Technology Report (pp. 113–119). https://www3.weforum.org/docs/GITR/2012/GITR_Chapter1.10_2012.pdf

Gajdzik, B., & Grabowska, S. (2018). Modele biznesowe w przedsiębiorstwach 4.0 – Próba identyfikacji założeń użytych do wyznaczania nowych modeli biznesu. *Zarządzanie Przedsiębiorstwem, 21*(3), 2–8.

Gama, J. A. P. (2018, October 3–6). Intelligent educational dual architecture for university digital transformation [Conference session]. *Proceedings of the 2018 IEEE Frontiers in Education Conference* (pp. 1–9), San Jose, CA.

Gehrke, S. (2014). The idea of the digital university: Ancient traditions, disruptive technologies and the Battle for the soul of higher education [Book Review, by F. B. McCluskey and M. L. Winter]. *The Review of Higher Education, 37*(4), 565–567.

Gilleard, C. (2017). The place of age in the digital revolution. In *Digital technologies and generational identity* (pp. 11–22). Routledge.

Gobble, M. M. (2018). Digital strategy and digital transformation. *Research-Technology Management, 61*(5), 66–71.

González, A. G. (2005). Open science: Open source licenses in scientific research. *North Carolina Journal of Law & Technology, 7*(2), 321.

Griffiths, J. (2013). Dematerialization, pragmatism and the European copyright revolution. *Oxford Journal of Legal Studies, 33*(4), 767–790.

Hadad, S., & Bratianu, C. (2019). Dematerialization of banking products and services in the digital era. *Management & Marketing, 14*(3)), 318–337.

Hammer, M., & Champy, J. (2009). *Reengineering the corporation: A manifesto for business revolution*. Zondervan.

Hassan, R. (2017). The worldly space: The digital university in network time. *British Journal of Sociology of Education, 38*(1), 72–82.

Hazemi, R., & Hailes, S. (Eds.). (2001). *The digital university-building: A learning community*. Springer Science & Business Media.

Hazemi, R., Hailes, S., & Wilbur, S. (Eds.). (2012). *The digital university: Reinventing the academy*. Springer Science & Business Media.

Heim, I., Han, T., & Ghobadian, A. (2018). Value co-creation in ICT services company: A case study of a cross-border acquisition. *Journal of East-West Business, 24*(4), 319–338.

Hess, T., Matt, C., Benlian, A., & Wiesböck, F. (2016). Options for formulating a digital transformation strategy. *MIS Quarterly Executive, 15*(2), 123–139.

Hinings, B., Gegenhuber, T., & Greenwood, R. (2018). Digital innovation and transformation: An institutional perspective. *Information and Organization, 28*(1), 52–61.

Hopkins, S. (2015). Ghosts in the machine: Incarcerated students and the digital university. *Australian Universities' Review, 57*(2), 46–53.

Hurd, F., & Singh, S. (2020). 'Something has to change': A collaborative journey towards academic well-being through critical reflexive practice. *Management Learning, 52*(3), 347–363.

Innes, J., & Booher, D. E. (1999). *Planning institutions in the network society: Theory for collaborative planning.* University of California at Berkeley, Institute of Urban and Regional Development.

Ismail, A. R., Nguyen, B., & Melewar, T. C. (2018). Impact of perceived social media marketing activities on brand and value consciousness: Roles of usage, materialism and conspicuous consumption. *International Journal of Internet Marketing and Advertising, 12*(3), 233–254.

Gandomani, T. J., & Ziaei, M. N. (2016). Agile transition and adoption human-related challenges and issues. *Computers in Human Behavior, 62*(C), 257–266.

Jewitt, C. (2013). Multimodal methods for researching digital technologies. *The SAGE handbook of digital technology research* (pp. 250–265). SAGE Publications Ltd.

Johnston, B., MacNeill, S., & Smyth, K. (Eds.). (2018a). Academic development for the digital university. In *Conceptualising the digital university* (pp. 217–233). Palgrave Macmillan.

Johnston, B., MacNeill, S., & Smyth, K. (Eds.). (2018b). Exploring the digital university: Developing and applying holistic thinking. In *Conceptualising the digital university* (pp. 39–60). Palgrave Macmillan.

Johnston, B., MacNeill, S., & Smyth, K. (Eds.). (2018c). Neoliberalism and the digital university: The political economy of learning in the twenty-first century. In *Conceptualising the digital university* (pp. 3–17). Palgrave Macmillan.

Johnston, B., MacNeill, S., & Smyth, K. (Eds.). (2018d). Neoliberalism and the digital university: The political economy of learning in the twenty-first century. In *Conceptualising the digital university* (pp. 3–17). Palgrave Macmillan.

Jones, C. (2013). The digital university: A concept in need of definition. In *Literacy in the digital university* (pp. 176–186). Routledge.

Kane, G. C., Palmer, D., Phillips, A. N., Kiron, D., & Buckley, N. (2015). Strategy, not technology, drives digital transformation. MIT Sloan Management Review and Deloitte University Press (pp. 1–25). https://www.cubility.com.au/wp-content/uploads/2018/11/dup_strategy-not-technology-drives-digital-transformation.pdf

Kenchakkanavar, A. Y. (2015). Facebook and Twitter for academic libraries in the twenty first century. *International Research: Journal of Library and Information Science, 5*(1), 162–173.

Khalid, J., Ram, B. R., Soliman, M., Ali, A. J., Khaleel, M., & Islam, M. S. (2018). Promising digital university: A pivotal need for higher education transformation. *International Journal of Management in Education, 12*(3), 264–275.

Kim, C., Yang, K. H., & Kim, J. (2008). A strategy for third-party logistics systems: A case analysis using the blue ocean strategy. *Omega, 36*(4), 522–534.

Knell, M. (2021). The digital revolution and digitalized network society. *Review of Evolutionary Political Economy, 2*(1), 9–25.

Kohtamäki, M., Thorgren, S., & Wincent, J. (2016). Organizational identity and behaviors in strategic networks. *Journal of Business & Industrial Marketing, 31*(1), 36–46.

Kokkinakos, P., Markaki, O., Koussouris, S., & Psarras, J. (2016, June). Digital transformation: Is public sector following the Enterprise 2.0 paradigm? In *International conference on digital transformation and global society* (pp. 96–105). Springer.

Kolbachev, E., & Kolbacheva, T. (2018, July). Human factor and working out of NBIC technologies. In *International conference on applied human factors and ergonomics* (pp. 179–190). Springer.

Krehbiel, T. C., Salzarulo, P. A., Cosmah, M. L., Forren, J., Gannod, G., Havelka, D., Hulshult, D., & Merhout, J. (2017). Agile manifesto for teaching and learning. *Journal of Effective Teaching, 17*(2), 90–111.

Kucia, M., Hajduk, G., Mazurek, G., & Kotula, N. (2021). The implementation of new technologies in customer value management—A sustainable development perspective. *Sustainability, 13*(2), 469.

Kulikowski, K., Przytuła, S., & Sułkowski, Ł (2021). The motivation of academics in remote teaching during the Covid-19 pandemic in Polish universities: Opening the Debate on a New Equilibrium in e-Learning. *Sustainability, 13*(5), 2752.

Laalo, H., Kinnari, H., & Silvennoinen, H. (2019). Setting new standards for homo academicus: Entrepreneurial university graduates on the EU agenda. *European Education, 51*(2), 93–110.

Lacković, N. (Ed.). (2020). Neoliberal higher education: Digital, innovative, relational, pictorial? In *Inquiry graphics in higher education* (pp. 25–43). Palgrave Macmillan.

Larsson, A., & Teigland, R. (2019). *Digital transformation and public services: Societal impacts in Sweden and beyond* (p. 378). Taylor & Francis.

Lasi, H., Fettke, P., Kemper, H. G., Feld, T., & Hoffmann, M. (2014). Industry 4.0. *Business & Information Systems Engineering, 6*(4), 239–242.

Liesner, A. (2006). Education or service? Remarks on teaching and learning in the entrepreneurial university. *Educational Philosophy and Theory, 38*(4), 483–495.

Lim, T. W. (Ed.). (2019). Digital disruptions and the workplace. In *Industrial revolution 4.0, tech giants, and digitized societies* (pp. 15–32). Palgrave Macmillan.

Lorenzo, N., & Gallon, R. (2019). Smart pedagogy for smart learning. In *Didactics of smart pedagogy* (pp. 41–69). Springer.

Losh, E. (2014). *The war on learning: Gaining ground in the digital university*. MIT Press.

Lu, T., Guo, X., Xu, B., Zhao, L., Peng, Y., & Yang, H. (2013, September). Next big thing in big data: The security of the ICT supply chain. *2013 International Conference on Social Computing* (pp. 1066–1073).

Lundberg, H., & Öberg, C. (2021). Digital university-SME interaction for business development. In *Impact of globalization and advanced technologies on online business models* (pp. 55–71). IGI Global.

MacNeill, S., Johnston, B., & Smyth, K. (2020). Critical engagement for active participation: The digital university in an age of populism. *New Directions for Adult & Continuing Education, 2020*(165), 115–127.

MacNeill, S., Smyth, K., & Johnston, B. (2015, June 9–12). Constructing the digital university—Open, collaborative models for strategic pedagogic and technical change. *Proceedings of the European Distance and E-Learning Network 2015 Annual Conference*, Barcelona, Spain.

Malar, D. A., Arvidsson, V., & Holmstrom, J. (2019). Digital transformation in banking: Exploring value co-creation in online banking services in India. *Journal of Global Information Technology Management, 22*(1), 7–24.

Maltese, V. (2018). Digital transformation challenges for universities: Ensuring information consistency across digital services. *Cataloging & Classification Quarterly, 56*(7), 592–606.

Matt, C., Hess, T., & Benlian, A. (2015). Digital transformation strategies. *Business & Information Systems Engineering, 57*(5), 339–343.

McAfee, A., Brynjolfsson, E., Davenport, T. H., Patil, D. J., & Barton, D. (2012). Big data: The management revolution. *Harvard Business Review, 90*(10), 60–68.

McCluskey, F. B., & Winter, M. L. (2012). *The idea of the digital university: Ancient traditions, disruptive technologies and the battle for the soul of higher education*. Westphalia Press.

McCluskey, F. B., & Winter, M. L. (2014). Academic freedom in the digital age. *On the Horizon, 22*(2), 136–146.

McQuade, S., Waitman, R., Zeisser, M., & Kierzkowski, A. (1996). Marketing to the digital consumer. *The McKinsey Quarterly*, (3), 4–5.

Mergel, I., Kattel, R., Lember, V., & McBride, K. (2018, May). Citizen-oriented digital transformation in the public sector. *Proceedings of the 19th Annual International Conference on Digital Government Research: Governance in the Data Age* (pp. 1–3), Delft, Netherlands.

Mihardjo, L. W. W., Sasmoko, Alamsjah, F., & Elidjen (2019). Digital transformation: A transformational performance-based conceptual model through co-creation strategy and business model innovation in the Industry 4.0 in Indonesia. *International Journal of Economics and Business Research, 18*(3), 369–386.

Mitchell, B. R. (Ed.). (2002). The relevance and impact of collaborative working for management in a digital university. In *The digital university—Building a learning community* (pp. 229–246). Springer.

Morrar, R., Arman, H., & Mousa, S. (2017). The fourth industrial revolution (Industry 4.0): A social innovation perspective. *Technology Innovation Management Review, 7*(11), 12–20.

Mosteanu, N. R. (2020a). Digital university Campus–Change the education system approach to meet the 21st century needs. *European Journal of Human Resource Management Studies, 4*(4), 79–92.

Mosteanu, N. R. (2020b). Using Internet and Edutech become a primary need rather than a luxury-the reality: a new skilled educational system-digital university campus. *International Journal of Engineering Science Technologies, 4*(6), 1–9.

Moutinho, J. L., & Heitor, M. (2007). Building human-centered systems in the network society. *Technological Forecasting and Social Change, 74*(1), 100–109.

Mu, J., Tang, F., & MacLachlan, D. L. (2010). Absorptive and disseminative capacity: Knowledge transfer in intra-organization networks. *Expert Systems with Applications, 37*(1), 31–38.

Munafò, M. R., Nosek, B. A., Bishop, D. V. M., Button, K. S., Chambers, C. D., Percie Du Sert, N., Simonsohn, U., Wagenmakers, E.-J., Ware, J. J., & Ioannidis., J. P. A. (2017). A manifesto for reproducible science. *Nature Human Behaviour, 1*(1), 1–9.

Nambisan, S., Wright, M., & Feldman, M. (2019). The digital transformation of innovation and entrepreneurship: Progress, challenges and key themes. *Research Policy, 48*(8), 103773.

Nicholas, D., Rowlands, I., Withey, R., & Dobrowolski, T. (2008). The digital consumer: An introduction and philosophy. In D. Nicholas & I. Rowlands (Eds.). *Digital consumers: Reshaping the information professions* (pp. 1–13). Facet.

Nicholas, D., & Rowlands, I. (Eds.). (2008). *Digital consumers: Reshaping the information professions*. Facet.

Pacholak, A. (2020). Digital university from student perspective: A step forward. *European Journal of Higher Education IT*. https://www.eunis.org/download/2020/EUNIS_2020_paper_10.pdf

Peters, M. A., Besley, T., Jandrić, P., & Neilson, X. Z. (2020). The democratic socialisation of knowledge: Integral to an alternative to the neoliberal model of development. In Neilson, D. (Ed.), *Knowledge socialism—The rise of peer production: Collegiality, collaboration, and collective intelligence* (pp. 135–154). Springer.

Peters, M. A., & Jandrić, P. (2018). Peer production and collective intelligence as the basis for the public digital university. *Educational Philosophy and Theory, 50*(13), 1271–1284.

Peters, M. A. (2012). Managerialism and the neoliberal university: Prospects for new forms of 'open management' in higher education. In M. A. Peters, T. C. Liu, & D. J. Ondercin (Eds.), *The pedagogy of the open society: Knowledge and the governance of higher education* (pp. 91–104). Brill Sense.

Pillania, R. K., & Chang, J. (2009). Research note: Global innovation and knowledge scenario: The stars, followers and laggards. *International Journal of Technology and Globalisation, 4*(4), 318–326.

Puriwat, W., & Tripopsakul, S. (2021). Customer engagement with digital social responsibility in social media: A case study of COVID-19 situation in Thailand. *The Journal of Asian Finance, Economics, and Business, 8*(2), 475–483.

Pynnönen, M., Ritala, P., & Hallikas, J. (2011). The new meaning of customer value: a systemic perspective. *Journal of Business Strategy, 32*(1), 51–57.

Quattrociocchi, B., Calabrese, M., Hysa, X., & Wankowicz, E. (2017). Technology and innovation for networks. *Journal of Organisational Transformation & Social Change, 14*(1), 4–20.

Raffaghelli, J. E., Cucchiara, S., Manganello, F., & Persico, D. (2016). Different views on digital scholarship: Separate worlds or cohesive research field? *Research in Learning Technology, 24*(1), 1–17.

Rakonjac, I., & Jednak, J. (2012). Sinergy of digital university and digital enterprise: Management of innovative activities. *Moving PM Competence Forward, 2*(1), 46–61.

Reddy, S. K., & Reinartz, W. (2017). Digital transformation and value creation: Sea change ahead. *Marketing Intelligence Review, 9*(1), 10–17.

Reis, J., Amorim, M., Melão, N., & Matos, P. (2018, March). Digital transformation: A literature review and guidelines for future research. In *World conference on information systems and technologies* (pp. 411–421). Springer.

Rhoads, R. A. (2018). A critical analysis of the development of the US research university and emergence of the neoliberal entrepreneurial model. *Entrepreneurship Education, 1*(1), 11–25.

Rigby, D. K., Sutherland, J., & Takeuchi, H. (2016). Embracing agile. *Harvard Business Review, 94*(5), 40–50.

Rodríguez-Haro, F., Freitag, F., Navarro, L., Hernánchez-sánchez, E., Farías-Mendoza, N., Guerrero-Ibáñez, J. A., & González-Potes, A. (2012). A summary of virtualization techniques. *Procedia Technology, 3*, 267–272.

Rohman, M., Marji, D. A. S., Sugandi, R. M., & Nurhadi, D. (2020). Online learning in higher education during Covid-19 pandemic: Students' perceptions. *Journal of Talent Development and Excellence, 12*(2s), 3644–3651.

Samaniego, M., & Deters, R. (2016). Management and Internet of Things. *Procedia Computer Science, 94*, 137–143.

Sandhu, G. (2018, February 21–23). The role of academic libraries in the digital transformation of the universities. *Proceedings of the 2018 5th International Symposium on Emerging Trends and Technologies in Libraries and Information Services* (pp. 292–296), Noida, India.

Sangster, A., Stoner, G., & Flood, B. (2020). Insights into accounting education in a COVID-19 world. *Accounting Education, 29*(5), 431–562.

Saxena, D. (2021). Big data for digital transformation of public services. In K. Sandhu (Ed.), *Disruptive technology and digital transformation for business and government* (pp. 250–266). IGI Global.

Schmitt, U. (2018). Rationalizing a personalized conceptualization for the digital transition and sustainability of knowledge management using the SVIDT method. *Sustainability, 10*(3), 839.

Sebastian, I. M., Ross, J. W., Beath, C., Mocker, M., Moloney, K. G., & Fonstad, N. O. (2020). How big old companies navigate digital transformation. In R. D. Galliers, D. E. Leidner, & B. Simeonova (Eds.), *Strategic information management* (pp. 133–150). Routledge.

Selwyn, N., Henderson, M., & Chao, S. H. (2018). 'You need a system': Exploring the role of data in the administration of university students and courses. *Journal of Further and Higher Education, 42*(1), 46–56.

Shao, X. F., Liu, W., Li, Y., Chaudhry, H. R., & Yue, X. G. (2021). Multistage implementation framework for smart supply chain management under industry 4.0. *Technological Forecasting and Social Change, 162*, 120354.

Sheail, P. (2018). Temporal flexibility in the digital university: Full-time, part-time, flexitime. *Distance Education, 39*(4), 462–479.

Shrouf, F., Ordieres, J., & Miragliotta, G. (2014, December). Smart factories in Industry 4.0: A review of the concept and of energy management approached in production based on the Internet of Things paradigm. *2014 IEEE International Conference on Industrial Engineering and Engineering Management* (pp. 697–701).

Siala, H. (2013). Crowdsourcing project management to the 'Open' Community. *PM World Journal, 10*(2), 1–17.

Simonette, M., Magalhães, M., & Spina, E. (2021). Digital transformation of academic management: All the tigers come at night. In D. Burgos & J. W. Branch *Radical solutions for digital transformation in Latin American universities* (pp. 77–92). Springer.

Sitnicki, M. (2018). Development of a model of digital research universities. *Baltic Journal of Economic Studies, 4*(1), 311–318.

Smyth, K., MacNeill, S., & Johnston, B. (2015). Visioning the digital University—From institutional strategy to academic practice. *Educational Developments, 16*(2), 13–17.

Strielkowski, W., & Wang, J. (2020, May). An introduction: COVID-19 pandemic and academic leadership. *6th International Conference on Social, Economic, and Academic Leadership (ICSEAL-6-2019)* (pp. 1–4).

Sullivan, C., & Staib, A. (2018). Digital disruption 'syndromes' in a hospital: Important considerations for the quality and safety of patient care during rapid digital transformation. *Australian Health Review, 42*(3), 294–298.

Sulkowski, L. (2022). Zarzadzanie uczelnia cyfrowa. Miedzy utopia wolnosci a dystopia wladzy, PWN, Warszawa, Polska.

Svensson, L., Öberg, L. M., & Olofsson, A. (2019, November 11–13). Towards excellence in flexible education: Identifying challenges for the digital university. *12th Annual International Conference of Education, Research and Innovation*, Seville, Spain (pp. 3223–3223).

Tabrizi, B., Lam, E., Girard, K., & Irvin, V. (2019). Digital transformation is not about technology. *Harvard Business Review, 13*(March), 1–6.

Tambotoh, J. J. C., Isa, S. M., Gaol, F. L., Soewito, B., & Warnars, H. L. H. S. (2016, October). Software quality model for Internet of Things governance. *2016 International Conference on Data and Software Engineering* (pp. 1–6).

Telli, S. G., & Aydin, S. (2021). Digitalization of marketing education: New approaches for universities in the post-Covid-19 era. *Üniversite Araştırmaları Dergisi, 4*(1), 61–74.

Uzzi, B. (1996). The sources and consequences of embeddedness for the economic performance of organizations: The network effect. *American Sociological Review, 61*(4), 674–698.

Van Der Merwe, D. (1999). The dematerialization of print and the fate of copyright. *International Review of Law, Computers & Technology, 13*(3), 303–315.

Van Dijk, J. A. (1999). The one-dimensional network society of Manuel Castells. *New media & Society, 1*(1), 127–138.

Velásquez, R. M. A., & Lara, J. V. M. (2021). Knowledge management in two universities before and during the COVID-19 effect in Peru. *Technology in Society, 64*, 101479.

Verdouw, C. N., Beulens, A. J., Reijers, H. A., & van der Vorst, J. G. (2015). A control model for object virtualization in supply chain management. *Computers Industry, 68*, 116–131.

Vial, G. (2019). Understanding digital transformation: A review and a research agenda. *The Journal of Strategic Information Systems, 28*(2), 118–144.

Vicente-Saez, R., & Martinez-Fuentes, C. (2018). Open science now: A systematic literature review for an integrated definition. *Journal of Business Research, 88*, 428–436.

Volkova, V. N., Kozlov, V. N., Karlik, A. E., & Iakovleva, E. A. (2017, November). The impact of NBIC-technology development on engineering and management personnel training. *2017 IEEE VI Forum Strategic Partnership of Universities and Enterprises of Hi-Tech Branches (Science. Education. Innovations)* (pp. 51–54).

Yao, L., Sheng, Q. Z., & Dustdar, S. (2015). Web-based management of the Internet of Things. *IEEE Internet Computing, 19*(4), 60–67.

Yu, E. S., & Mylopoulus, J. (1996). Using goals, rules and methods to support reasoning in business process reengineering. *Intelligent Systems in Accounting, Finance & Management, 5*(1), 1–13.

Zain, S. (2021). Digital transformation trends in education. In D. Baker, & L. Ellis (Eds.), *Future directions in digital information* (pp. 223–234). Chandos Publishing.

Zhang, X., van Donk, D. P., & van Der Vaart, T. (2011). Does ICT influence supply chain management and performance? A review of survey-based research. *International Journal of Operations & Production Management, 31*(11), 1215–1247.

Zhao, M., Liao, H.-T., & Sun, S.-P. (2020, April 10–12). An education literature review on digitization, digitalization, datafication, and digital transformation. *Proceedings of the 6th International Conference on Humanities and Social Science Research*, Hangzhou, China.

Zwick, D., & Dholakia, N. (2004). Consumer subjectivity in the age of Internet: The radical concept of marketing control through customer relationship management. *Information and Organization, 14*(3), 211–236.

2 Digital Innovations
A New Direction for Higher Education

Regina Lenart-Gansiniec

2.1 Basic Information about Innovations

The concept of the word "innovation" is derived from the Latin word "innovare", which means to renew, create new things or change. The first scholar to introduce the theory of innovation was J. Schumpeter (Fagerberg, 2003) who recognized that innovation comes down to introducing a new production method, opening a new market, acquiring a new source of raw materials or semi-finished products or introducing a new organization of an industry. It is, therefore, related to the introduction of a new solution into the practice of organization. In turn, the Organization for Economic Co-operation and Development (OECD) published in 1992 the "Oslo Manual: Proposed Guidelines for Collecting and Interpreting Technological Innovation Data", which was updated in 1997, 2005 and 2018. According to that publication:

> innovation results from knowledge-based activities, which consist in the practical application of existing or newly created information and knowledge. Information consists of structured data and can be duplicated and transferred between organizations at low cost. Knowledge refers to understanding information and the ability to use information for different purposes. Knowledge is obtained through cognitive effort, and thus new knowledge is difficult to convey as it requires learning from the recipient. Both information and knowledge can be acquired or created inside, or outside a given organization.
> Oslo Manual; OECD/Eurostat, 2018, p. 50

In this approach, innovation means implementation of a new organizational method in the firm's business practices, workplace organization or external relations.

In turn, Chen and Yin (2019, p. 27) have thoroughly revised the definition of the definition. According to their findings: "American scholar Mansfield believed that an invention could be termed a technological innovation the first time it was applied (Mansfield, 1968). British technology

DOI: 10.4324/9781003227175-3

policy expert Prof. Christopher Freeman considered innovation to involve many steps (e.g., technology, design, manufacturing, finance, management and marketing) that took place the first time a new product to process was initiated (Freeman, 1987). American scholar Chesbrough defined innovation as the creation and commercialization of an invention (Chesbrough, 2003). American scholar Drucker considered innovation to be a special tool an entrepreneur applies in order to turn changes into different business and service opportunities. Innovation can be a discipline, an academic field or a practice" (Drucker, 2009). Generally speaking, innovation means the implementation of a new or significantly improved product (product or service) or process, a new marketing method or a new organizational method in economic practice, workplace organization or relations with the environment.

However, it should be emphasized that innovation should not be combined with creativity (Amabile et al., 1996). Creativity can be understood as a psychological process, part of human intelligence and cognitive abilities. In this conceptualization, creativity is based on emotions, the joy of creating something new and tolerating ambiguous answers and solutions, which translates into the readiness and ability to formulate new problems, communicate and apply knowledge in various contexts. Thus, creativity in psychological terms is a certain attitude and the resultant of skills, expert knowledge, intelligence, talent, cognitive and personality processes, cognitive style, internal motivation to undertake tasks, interests, pleasure, a sense of challenge, passion and external motivators. Creativity is perceived as the cause of action and creation, as well as the process of communicating innovation with the environment. This involves stimulating new thoughts, reformulating existing knowledge and analysing assumptions to form new ideas. It can, therefore, be concluded that creativity stimulates the creation of innovation.

Innovations can be divided into several categories. In particular, product innovations, process innovations, service innovation and business model innovation can be distinguished. Following the Oslo Manual (OECD/Eurostat, 2018), a product innovation is a new or improved product or service that differs significantly from the company's existing products or services, and which has been introduced to the market. Product innovation must result in a significant improvement to one or more properties or performance specifications. Relevant functional characteristics in this case include quality, technical specifications, reliability, durability, economy in use, affordability, convenience, usability and user-friendliness. Product innovation does not have to be associated with the improvement of all functions and performance specifications. When you upgrade or add a new feature, you may lose other features or decrease performance in some respects. Product innovation may require supportive innovation in the business process. This situation is particularly common in the case of service innovation. If this innovation leads to the creation of a new sales channel for the first time, it can also be considered a marketing innovation.

Process innovation refers to a new or improved business process for one or more business functions that differs significantly from the company's existing business processes and that has been put into use by the enterprise. The corresponding features of the enhanced business function are related to the features of the enhanced product, in particular, the services that can be provided to business customers. Examples include increased efficiency, resource efficiency, reliability, affordability, convenience and usability for those involved in the business process, both outside and inside the enterprise.

Service innovation comes down to design, development and service provision, and changes to solve customer problems. It comes down to new distribution channels, new ways of interacting with customers, new features that are important both for service providers and for customers. Such innovations are related to creation of new value for customers. In addition, service innovation is the result of a change process or the product-related process itself, characterized by a high degree of immateriality and the need for contact between the service provider and the customer.

Finally, business model innovation refers to changes in the ways of creating value for customers, in particular in terms of their needs, as well as the entry of organizations into new markets and acquiring new customers. It is also exploring new ways to generate cash flows (Sorescu et al., 2011). At the same time, the business model is a kind of summary of what is the set of interrelated decision variables in the area of strategy, business configuration and economic benefits intended to create a lasting competitive advantage in specific markets. In this approach, "the business model is a conceptual tool that contains a series of elements and their relationships that shed light on the business logic of a particular entity. It describes the value companies can provide to their customers, as well as the company's internal structure, partner networks and relationship capital to achieve (create, market and deliver) this value and generate sustainable, profitable revenue" (Osterwalder & Pigneur, 2010).

Innovation in education systems can be understood as "the adoption of new services, technologies, competences by educational organizations" that "can help to improve learning outcomes, strengthen equity and improve efficiency" (European Commission, 2018, p. 2). Consequently, the Digital Education Action Plan (European Commission, 2018) identifies three key policy priorities: (1) making better use of digital technologies in teaching and learning, (2) developing relevant digital competences and skills for digital transformation and (3) improving education through better data analysis and forecasting.

2.2 Digital Orientation

The very term "digital" comes down to the use of digital technology in a wide range of innovation, the conversion of mainly analogue information into binary language understood by computers and broadband infrastructure enabling access to high-speed Internet (Nabisan et al., 2017). The concept of orientation is defined as leaning towards something, gravitating towards a certain direction. It is also the state of the subject of action, who knows the circumstances in view of its potential, i.e., knows the conditions and knows whether they can achieve their goal, and if so, how, when, with whose help. Orientation is, therefore, an act, a process of orientation. In this approach, strategic orientation comes down to managerial choices made in order to achieve the desired business goals (Leskovar-Spacapan & Bastic, 2007) and defines the behaviour of the organization in relation to the subsystems of the organization, as well as the ideas and beliefs of management about organizational processes covering the above-mentioned dimensions (Venkatraman, 1989) and the strategic directions set by the organization to create behaviours that lead to the highest performance (Narver & Slater, 1990). Strategic orientation reflects the company's philosophy of doing business through a deeply ingrained set of values and beliefs that guide the company's attempt to achieve top performance (Gatignon & Xuereb, 1997). Strategic orientations represent valuable intangible abilities that are difficult to imitate and provide a sustainable competitive advantage (Schweiger et al., 2019). Strategic orientation is an indication of the direction in which an organization wants or should go in the future. Strategic orientation helps the organization to analyse the strategy, influences the organization's ability to succeed and its innovativeness (Narver & Slater, 1990). Organizations with strategic orientation are proactive, willing to take risks and make better use of their resources. Strategic orientations result from a process of cultural and behavioural transformation that reflects external factors such as competition dynamics (Theodosiou et al., 2012) as well as internal factors such as focus on top management, interdepartmental collaboration and reward systems (Gebhardt et al., 2006).

There are four dominant strategies in the literature, such as: market orientation (e.g., Narver & Slater, 1990), learning orientation (e.g., Sinkula et al., 1997) and entrepreneurship orientation (e.g., Covin & Slevin, 1989). Market orientation focuses on creating and delivering value for the customer (Lonial & Carter, 2015) and aims at collecting and disseminating market information (Kohli & Jaworski, 1990). Learning orientation refers to an organization's ability to generate and use knowledge to improve its competitive advantage (Calantone et al., 2002). Learning orientation affects the way knowledge is acquired and interpreted. Entrepreneurship orientation reflects the organization's commitment to innovative activities, its reactivity and risk taking (Wiklund & Shepherd, 2005).

Additionally, one of the strategic orientations refers to digital orientation involving changes caused by digital technology. Quinton et al. (2018) indicate that the digital orientation is the deliberate strategic positioning of organizations to take advantage of the opportunities presented by digital technologies. It, therefore, encompasses attitudes and behaviours that support the generation and use of market knowledge, proactive innovation and openness to new ideas, and fusion of the link between specific technology sets and organizational processes and procedures (Leonardi, 2011). Digital orientation involves the use of technology in various ways and through various means. These include, but are not limited to, customer-oriented digital technologies that include technical interfaces through which customers can access services that enable a standardized provision of services to provide greater flexibility of access. Accordingly, digitally oriented organizations are more open to the digitization of technology and have the competence to implement digital innovations.

2.3 Digital Capability

Competences are usually defined in the literature as the scope of powers and authorizations, authority, skills and responsibility. Competences also mean having knowledge and experience in a certain field, enabling the proper performance of duties and making the right decisions. Competencies are, therefore, a bundle of related knowledge, skills and abilities that influence a significant part of an individual's work, and they are correlated with the achievement of performance at work.

Construction of the concept of competence includes three elements: knowledge, skills and abilities. Knowledge relates to all the information acquired through research and learning. It is related to the possessed data, information, experience and education. Skills refer to practical knowledge of something, proficiency in performing certain activities. Abilities refer to action potential, regardless of their praxeological characteristics, i.e., for instance, the level of fitness. The concept is identified with cognitive dispositions focused on the reception and processing of a specific type of stimuli.

Generally speaking, it is a bundle, combination or set of individual potentials in the use of knowledge or skills to accomplish specific tasks. Competences include effective action in various areas of life through activities mobilized at the same time and in related ways, through elements of attitudes, procedures and concepts. Since this definition means taking effective actions in situations and various types of problems, the competences indicate the use of various resources. Competences are the resultant of knowledge, skills, abilities, tendencies and motivation to generate new, original, useful and effective ideas in terms of effectiveness and power.

Digital competences are knowledge, skills and attitudes that allow you to perform tasks, solve problems, communicate, manage information, cooperate, create and share content (Freel, 2005; Renko et al., 2009) effectively, correctly, safely, critically, creatively and ethically. It is also the organization's skills, talent and experience in managing digital technologies for the development of new product development (Carcary et al., 2016). Digital competences allow organizations for adapting to the requirements, expectations and needs of the society, for improving employability and higher skills in the digital economy, attracting more students in the global education market, improving processes, systems and building organizational capacity, maximizing the value of investments in technologies, content and educational services, and providing high-quality education in a flexible and innovative way.

Digital competences include the following: ICT proficiency, information, data and media literacy, digital creation, problem solving and innovation, digital communication, collaboration and participation, digital learning and development, and digital identity (Levallet & Chan, 2018):

- ICT proficiency – the capacity to use ICT-based devices, applications, software and services via their interfaces (mouse, keyboard, touch screen, voice control and other modes of input; screens, microphones, haptic feedback and other modes of output); to use basic productivity software, web browser and writing/presentation software; to use digital capture devices such as a camera. At higher levels, the capacity: to choose, adapt and personalize ICT applications and systems; to critically assess the benefits/constraints of ICT applications and approaches; to design and implement ICT solutions; to recover from failures; to stay up to date with ICT as it evolves; to adopt computational modes of thinking (coding, algorithms, etc).
- Data, media and information literacy – information literacy (the capacity to find, evaluate, manage, curate, organize and share digital information, including open content. At higher levels a critical awareness of provenance and credibility. Capacity to interpret information for academic and professional/vocational purposes. Ability to act within the rules of copyright and to use appropriate referencing. Ability to record and preserve information for future access and use). Media literacy (the capacity to critically read communications in a range of digital media – text, graphical, video, animation, audio, haptic, etc (also "multimodal literacy"). At higher levels, the capacity to appreciate audience, purpose, accessibility, impact, modality and to understand digital media production as a practice and an industry. Data literacy (the capacity to collate, manage, access and use digital data in spreadsheets and other media; to record and use personal data; to ensure data security and to use legal, ethical and security guidelines in data collection and use. At higher levels the ability to interpret data by running queries, data analyses and reports).
- Digital creation, scholarship and innovation (creative production) – digital creation (the capacity to design and/or create new digital artefacts and materials; digital writing; digital imaging; digital editing of images, video and audio. At higher levels the ability to code and to design apps/applications, games, virtual environments and interfaces). Digital research and scholarship (the capacity to collect and

analyse research data using digital methods. At higher levels to discover, develop and share new ideas using digital tools; to undertake open scholarship; to design new research questions and programmes around digital issues/methods; to develop new digital tools/processes; to evaluate impacts of digital interventions). Digital innovation (the capacity to develop new practices with digital technology in organizational settings and in specialist subject areas (professional, vocational and disciplinary); digital entrepreneurship. At higher levels the ability to lead organizations, departments, teams and practice/subject areas in new directions in response to digital challenges and opportunities).
- Digital communication, collaboration and participation (participating) – digital communication (the capacity to communicate effectively in a variety of digital media and digital forums; to communicate in accordance with different cultural, social and communicational norms; to design communications for different purposes and audiences; to respect others in public communications; to maintain privacy in private communications). Digital collaboration (the capacity to participate in digital teams and working groups; to collaborate effectively using shared digital tools and media; to work towards shared objectives; to produce shared materials; to use shared calendars and task lists and other project management applications; to work effectively across cultural, social and linguistic boundaries). Digital participation (the capacity to participate in, facilitate and build digital networks; to participate in social and cultural life using digital services and forums; to create positive connections and build contacts; to share and amplify messages across networks; to behave safely and ethically in networking situations).
- Digital learning and personal/professional development (learning) – the capacity to identify and participate in digital learning opportunities; to use digital learning resources; to participate in learning/teaching relationships via digital media; to use digital tools (personal or organizational) for learning; to use digital tools to organize, plan and reflect on learning; to record learning events/data and use them for self-analysis, reflection and showcasing of achievement; to undertake self-assessment and participate in other forms of digital assessment; to manage attention and motivation to learn in digital settings.
- Digital identity and wellbeing (self-actualizing) – digital identity management (the capacity to develop and project a positive digital identity or identities and to manage digital reputation (personal or organizational) across a range of platforms; to build and maintain digital profiles; to develop a personal style and values for digital participation; to collate and curate personal materials across digital networks). Digital wellbeing (the capacity to look after personal health, safety, relationships and work-life balance in digital settings; to use personal digital data for positive wellbeing benefits; to use digital media to

foster community actions and wellbeing; to act safely and responsibly in digital environments; to manage digital stress, workload and distraction; to act with concern for the human and natural environment when using digital tools; to balance digital with real-world interactions appropriately – see: https://digitalcapability.jiscinvolve.org/wp/files/2015/06/1.-Digital-capabilities-6-elements.pdf.

2.4 Digital Innovation in HEI

Digital innovation refers to innovative information and technology solutions that integrate digital technologies to support digitization of organizations. Digital innovation refers to coordinated orchestration of new products, new processes, new services, new platforms and even new business models in a given context (Nambisan et al., 2017). It is also development of new products, services or solutions using digital technology. Digital innovations are characterized by the following features (Yoo et al., 2010): (1) reprogrammability (2) homogenization of data and (3) self-referential nature of digital technology. This means that through digital innovation, an organization can involve its customers in co-designing products or services. From the organizational point of view, the benefits include the following: increased productivity, improved access to customers, implementation of new products or services, lower operating costs (Boss et al., 2007), as well as the possibility of creating new types of innovative processes (Henfridsson et al., 2014).

The digital technology used in innovation includes: crowd-based digital innovation, big data, Internet of Things (IoT), cloud computing, augmented and virtual reality, artificial intelligence (AI) and cyber-physical systems (Urbinati et al., 2019):

- Crowd-based digital innovation refers to the use of digital technologies to engage a range of stakeholders in generating innovative solutions to the problem (Dahlander et al., 2019; Majchrzak & Malhotra, 2020; Tucci et al., 2018).
- Big data refers to the combination of structured, semi-structured and unstructured data collected by organizations that can be mined for information and used in machine learning projects, predictive modelling and other advanced analytical applications. In this approach, big data is a large amount of data in many environments, a wide range of data types often stored in big data systems, and the speed with which most data is generated, collected and processed.
- IoT refers to a system of interrelated Internet-connected objects that are able to collect and transmit data over a wireless network without human intervention. The term is associated with radio frequency identification as a method of communication, but also includes other sensor technologies, wireless technologies or QR codes.

- Cloud computing comes down to the use of external systems that help computers store, manage, process and/or transmit information. These external systems are hosted in the cloud. They can include everything from email servers to computer programs, data storage and even increasing the processing power of a computer. In short, this means storing and accessing data and programs over the Internet instead of on your computer's hard drive.
- Augmented reality refers to an improved version of the real physical world that is achieved through the use of digital visual elements, sound or other sensory stimuli provided through technology. So, it consists in superimposing visual, auditory or other sensory information into the world in order to enhance the experience.
- Virtual reality is a term used to describe a three-dimensional, computer-generated environment that can be explored and interacted with. Refers to computer-generated or reality environments that are intended to simulate the physical presence of a person in a particular environment, intended to appear real. The purpose of virtual reality is to enable a person to experience and manipulate the environment as if it were the real world.
- Artificial intelligence is a wide-ranging branch of computer science dedicated to building intelligent machines capable of performing tasks that typically require human intelligence. It refers to the simulation of human intelligence processes by machines, especially computer systems. Specific AI applications include expert systems, natural language processing, speech recognition and machine vision.
- Cyber-physical systems come down to the integration of computing, network and physical processes. Embedded computers and networks monitor and control physical processes through feedback loops where physical processes influence computation and vice versa. They involve some interaction of digital, analogue, physical and human components designed to operate through integrated physics and logic.

In the context of universities, digital innovations can take of the following forms: massive online open classes (MOOC), the digital educational resources engine: an innovation for accessibility to knowledge, self-assessment tests: an educational innovation designed for participative teaching, computer simulation: an innovation for learning in real-life situations in the medical and paramedical field and dematerializing the credentials: the certification of diplomas using the blockchain.

- MOOC – online courses open to all, offered by HEIs around the world. These are free trainings that allow any interested person for participating without any pre-set conditions. Certain courses offer a certification system in return for a financial contribution. Course topics often vary from math to social sciences, personal development and health.

- The digital educational resources engine – an innovation for accessibility to knowledge – refers to digital libraries that bring together a variety of educational resources, such as electronic journals, e-books, digitized traditional paper publications (magazines, books, maps, photos, etc.).
- Self-assessment tests – an assessment tool used to assess the quality of work undertaken, measure performance against defined learning goals and objectives, identify work related strengths and weaknesses and implement revisions appropriately. This digital innovation enables students to self-evaluate and the teacher to check that students follow and understand the course concepts.
- Computer simulation – using a computer to represent the dynamic responses of one system by the behaviour of another system modelled. The simulation uses a mathematical description or a model of the real system in the form of a computer program. Computer simulation allows for virtual prediction of real cases that might be met in working life. These are real situations that teach students to react to serious or less serious situations.
- Dematerializing the credentials (certification of diplomas using the blockchain) – a distributed database that is shared by computer network nodes. As a database, the blockchain stores information electronically in the digital format. This also refers to an expanding list of cryptographically signed irrevocable transaction records shared by all network participants. Each record includes a timestamp and links to previous transactions. This information allows anyone with access rights for tracing the transaction event.

2.5 Drivers and Barriers of Digital Innovation in HEI

Digital innovations involve two categories: culture of openness and freedom and conscious innovation management. With regard to culture of openness and freedom, the following drivers can be distinguished: intensified local, regional and international cooperation across the higher education arena, strong cooperation established between HEIs and business, empowerment of employees and the decentralization of units, autonomous participatory governance model applied at HEIs, big proportion of teamwork and cross-faculty, cross-disciplinary cooperation of various organizational units, establishment of specialized cross-cutting workplaces, instilling an open communication climate, establishing regular meetings and communication channels across HEI, specialized platforms for exchange of best practices in regard to education among professionals from the academic community, involvement of students into decisional and management structures, and academic freedom regarding teachers' decisions on the study program content and methods used.

In the case of conscious innovation management, the following drivers are discussed in the literature: professional management-related best practices applied, detailed conscious strategic planning and vision for innovativeness, strategy and objectives directly linked to innovation, continuous quality assurance systems applied in each department at HEI, inclusion of the total quality management concept into management processes, HEIs' managers/leaders serving as role models for other employees in innovativeness, with primary role to provide contacts onto the business sphere, networking and verbalization of prominent innovative activities taking place at HEIs, massive emergence of new organizational structure-related positions and units that aim specifically at supporting the innovations in education, mergers of organizational units/faculties at HEIs, support to the HEIs' staff, especially in the form of training and development in order to compensate the raising pressure on staff to acquire skills related to new ICT tools, performance management practices: clear rules for staff evaluation, frequency of assessments, inclusion of innovative potential to the conditions and system of comprehensive evaluation of teachers, motivation through financial remuneration of innovators.

When it comes to barriers to implementation of digital innovations in HEI, three categories of obstacles are identified: (1) external barriers to innovation at the macro level, (2) internal barriers operating in the organizational environment of the participants and (3) barriers at the individual level of analyses related to the two main internal stakeholders of universities, i.e., teachers and students, and their reluctance to innovate and lack of ICT-related skills.

With regard to external barriers, the following can be indicated: lack of funds, high level of bureaucracy due to macro-level regulations, complicated and non-transparent administration, lack of transparency of information and clear accountability, lack of an educational development strategy, rigid and time-consuming public procurement procedures, low level of trust in the relationship between scientists and company owners/managers, poor interaction between the academic community and business, inconsistency in ICT tools and technologies used by various units/faculties at universities, mismatch between the fast pace of technological development and the time-consuming process of implementing tools and technologies ICT in universities.

Internal barriers include the following: insufficient empowerment of executive bodies at HEIs, slow decision-making process, unclear governance structures and related responsibilities and accountability of HEI's representatives, lack of coordination and communication from HEI's management to employees, lack of communication between different units and departments at faculties, inconsistent management practices across faculties and loosed-coupled management between different departments, conservative and bureaucratic organizational culture, inefficient utilization of financial resources, insufficient financial support for new emerging organizational units, lack of effective inspection that would aim at helping HEI's employees to improve their skills, lack of material, technical and technological equipment and support, remunerations that do not support innovations or innovation efforts that are just occasionally incentivized, job descriptions that do not delineate explicitly innovation-tied activities and responsibilities of employees, and work overload of the academic staff and poor planning and organization of work.

With regard to individual barriers, the following can be listed: prejudices against modernization, personal negative attitudes and resistance to change, fear, uncertainty as well as worries that things cannot be changed, lack of interest of more conservative teachers, obsolete forms, methods and procedures for evaluating students, lack of awareness about innovative ways of teaching, insufficient ICT-related skills, negative attitude toward innovations, indifferent approach and lack of interest in learning, lack of participation and involvement in the decision-making processes and governance functions at HEIs, and insufficient ICT-related skills (Lašáková et al., 2017).

2.6 Trends in Digital Innovation in HEI

Smart university is one the latest trends. The smart university concept assumes emergence of technologies based on the IoT (Tikhomirov et al., 2015). In other words, a smart university is a multi-subject configuration combining six areas, such as smart education, smart classroom, smart learning environments, smart campus, smart teacher and smart learning communities. Those elements of smart universities compiled together aim at interactive university management, a systemic approach to teaching, personalizing learning, efficiently managing a group of students and monitoring their progress.

Smart education can be defined as a multidisciplinary education system focused on students. Such education is related to the use of modern technology that facilitates communication, interaction, management and storage of knowledge (Coccoli et al., 2014). Intelligent education, therefore, includes solutions that improve communication, sharing resources between faculty and students, managing student affairs, including monitoring and reporting student results, and storing large resources of knowledge and enabling unlimited access to them. In practice, it comes down to the use of modern digital technologies and computerized administration, such as cloud and computer networks, next-generation telecommunications networks and mobile devices.

Smart classroom means the use of modern technologies that improve the display process, management, accessibility and interactivity when conducting classes with students (Pishva & Nishantha, 2008). Such solutions make it possible to optimize the presentation of teaching content, enable unlimited access to educational resources, distance learning using information and telecommunications techniques and the IoT technology (e.g., online videoconferencing, interactive television) (Huang & Rice, 2012).

The main purpose of implementing such solutions is to activate students, but also to change the way of thinking about education, which is supposed to help students acquire adaptive skills, logical reasoning, self-education and self-organization.

A smart learning environment supports students through the use of technologies that enable some analysis of their behaviour, performance and needs (Hwang, 2014). Due to such monitoring, students can receive help and feedback on results and achievements at any time. Therefore, an intelligent environment focuses on adapting education to the needs and abilities of learners involved. Lecturers, in turn, allow for identifying the learning style of students and developing an individualized and personalized method of working with them.

Smart campus in literature is defined as a new thinking paradigm relating to an environment including e-learning, collaborative networks, green and sustainable ICT development, management systems using sensors and automatic security control (Kwok, 2015). It is, therefore, a combination of an integrated cloud computing and the IoT (Xiao et al., 2013). In practice, it comes down to building management using the integration of electrical and power systems, audio–visual, lighting, telecommunications, IT, fire alarms, burglary alarms, internal transport, air conditioning and ventilation or heating.

Smart teachers refer to a strategy that includes facilities to support teachers in their work. All tools and technological innovations are primarily provided to facilitate assessment done by lecturers.

The smart learning environment is an environment focused on establishing communication with others, operating on the principle of reciprocity, cooperation, trust and gratitude with the maximum use of technology. This environment is aware of behaviour of all users in the learning process, and it helps in the exchange of educational content (Frankl & Bitter, 2013).

Smart university is a creative, sustainable university with comprehensive modernization of all processes and activities. It can be understood as the sum of technological improvements related to functioning of the university's infrastructure and resources, as well as services. Thanks to intelligent solutions implemented at university, it is also possible to simplify decision-making and administrative processes, which has a significant impact on building the image of a student-friendly university. Other benefits include modifying the scope of services offered in accordance with the expectations and preferences of students and creating a friendly space for their activity. This is especially noticeable in the innovative configurations of intelligent lecture rooms adapted to the needs of students and the design of classes rich in multimedia content, interactive presentations, quizzes, tests, and video lectures.

Crowdsourcing is one of the solutions that manifest digital innovation, but also fit into the idea of smart university. Moreover, the use of crowdsourcing in learning and teaching processes can lead to pedagogical innovation and the improvement of the learning and professional skills of students. Crowdsourcing promoters in HEIs are convinced that it can be useful for gaining ideas, opinions, feedback from the virtual community, gaining support for various projects, as well as improving communication between individual stakeholders, and even collecting data as part of scientific research, creating textbooks and raising funds for educational projects. In the case of the latter, it is indicated that the use of crowdsourcing allows for the optimization of the institution's budget and more effective use of time for study (Llorente & Morant, 2015).

References

Amabile, T. M., Conti, R., Coon, H., Lazenby, J., & Herron, M. (1996). Assessing the work environment for creativity. *Academy of Management Journal*, 39(5), 1154–1184.

G. Boss, P. Malladi, D. Quan, L. Legregni and H. Hall, *Cloud Computing*, IBM Corporation, New York, August 2007, http://www.ibm.com/developerswork/webspherezones/hipods/library.html.

Calantone, R. J., Cavusgil, S. T., & Zhao, Y. (2002). Learning orientation, firm innovation capability, and firm performance. *Industrial Marketing Management*, 31(6), 515–524.

Carcary, M., Doherty, E., & Conway, G. (2016, September). A dynamic capability approach to digital transformation: A focus on key foundational themes. *The European Conference on Information Systems Management* (p. 20), Evora, Portugal.

Chen, J., & Yin, X. (2019). Connotation and types of innovation. In J. Chen, A. Brem, E. Viardot, & P. K. Wong (Eds.), *The Routledge companion to innovation management* (pp. 26–54). Routledge.

Chesbrough, H. (2003). The logic of open innovation: Managing intellectual property. *California Management Review*, 45(3), 33–58.

Coccoli, M., Guercio, A., Maresca, P., & Stanganelli, L. (2014). Smarter universities: A vision for the fast changing digital era. *Journal of Visual Languages & Computing*, 25(6), 1003–1011.

European Commission (2018). Communication from the Commission to the European Parliament, the Council, the European Economic and Social Committee and the Committee of the Regions on the Digital Education Action Plan, https://eur-lex.europa.eu/legal-content/EN/TXT/PDF/?uri=CELEX:52018DC0022&from=EN

Covin, J. G., & Slevin, D. P. (1989). Strategic management of small firms in hostile and benign environments. *Strategic Management Journal*, 10(1), 75–87.

Dahlander, L., Jeppesen, L. B., & Piezunka, H. (2019). How organizations manage crowds: Define, broadcast, attract, and select. In J. Sydow, & H. Berends (Eds.), *Managing inter-organizational collaborations: Process views*. Emerald Publishing Limited.

Drucker, P. F. (2009). *Innovation and entrepreneurship* (Reprint ed.). HarperCollins e-books.

Fagerberg, J. (2003). Schumpeter and the revival of evolutionary economics: An appraisal of the literature. *Journal of Evolutionary Economics*, 13(2), 125–159.

Frankl, G., & Bitter, S. (2013, July). Collaboration is smart: Smart learning communities. In A. Holzinger, & G. Pasi (Eds.), *International workshop on human–computer interaction and knowledge discovery in complex, unstructured, big data* (pp. 293–302). Springer.

Freel, M. S. (2005). Patterns of innovation and skills in small firms. *Technovation*, 25(2), 123–134.

Freeman, C. (1987). Technical innovation, diffusion, and long cycles of economic development. In T. Vasko (Ed.), *The long-wave debate* (pp. 295–309). Springer.

Gatignon, H., & Xuereb, J. M. (1997). Strategic orientation of the firm and new product performance. *Journal of Marketing Research*, *34*(1), 77–90.

Gebhardt, G. F., Carpenter, G. S., & Sherry, J. F., Jr. (2006). Creating a market orientation: A longitudinal, multifirm, grounded analysis of cultural transformation. *Journal of Marketing*, *70*(4), 37–55.

Henfridsson, O., Mathiassen, L., & Svahn, F. (2014). Managing technological change in the digital age: The role of architectural frames. *Journal of Information Technology*, *29*(1), 27–43.

Huang, F., & Rice, J. (2012). Openness in product and process innovation. *International Journal of Innovation Management*, *16*(4), 1250020.

Hwang, G. J. (2014). Definition, framework and research issues of smart learning environments-a context-aware ubiquitous learning perspective. *Smart Learning Environments*, *1*(1), 1–14.

Kohli, A. K., & Jaworski, B. J. (1990). Market orientation: The construct, research propositions, and managerial implications. *Journal of Marketing*, *54*(2), 1–18.

Kwok, L. F. (2015). A vision for the development of i-campus. *Smart Learning Environments*, *2*(2), 1–12.

Lašáková, A., Remišová, A., & Kirchmayer, Z. (2017). Are managers in Slovakia ethical leaders? Key findings on the level of ethical leadership in the Slovak business environment. *Periodica Polytechnica Social and Management Sciences*, *25*(2), 87–96.

Leonardi, P. M. (2011). Innovation blindness: Culture, frames, and cross-boundary problem construction in the development of new technology concepts. *Organization Science*, *22*(2), 347–369.

Leskovar-Spacapan, G., & Bastic, M. (2007). Differences in organizations' innovation capability in transition economy: Internal aspect of the organizations' strategic orientation. *Technovation*, *27*(9), 533–546.

Levallet, N., & Chan, Y. E. (2018). Role of digital capabilities in unleashing the power of managerial improvisation. *MIS Quarterly Executive*, *17*(1), 4–21.

Llorente, R., & Morant, M. (2015). Crowdsourcing in higher education. In F. J. Garrigos-Simo, I. Gil-Pechuán, & S. Estelles-Miguel (Eds.), *Advances in crowdsourcing* (pp. 87–95). Springer.

Lonial, S. C., & Carter, R. E. (2015). The impact of organizational orientations on medium and small firm performance: A resource-based perspective. *Journal of Small Business Management*, *53*(1), 94–113.

Majchrzak, A., & Malhotra, A. (2020). *Unleashing the crowd*. Springer International Publishing.

Mansfield, E. (1968). *Industrial research and technological innovation: An econometric analysis*.

Nambisan, S., Lyytinen, K., Majchrzak, A., & Song, M. (2017). Digital innovation management: Reinventing innovation management research in a digital world. *MIS Quarterly*, *41*(1), 223–238.

Narver, J. C., & Slater, S. F. (1990). The effect of a market orientation on business profitability. *Journal of Marketing*, *54*(4), 20–35.

OECD/Eurostat. (2018). *Oslo Manual 2018: Guidelines for collecting, reporting and using data on innovation* (4th ed.). OECD Publishing

Osterwalder, A., & Pigneur, Y. (2010). *Business model generation: A handbook for visionaries, game changers, and challengers* (Vol. 1). John Wiley & Sons.

Pishva, D., & Nishantha, G. G. D. (2008). Smart classrooms for distance education and their adoption to multiple classroom architecture. *Journal of Networks, 3*(5), 54–64.

Quinton, S., Canhoto, A., Molinillo, S., Pera, R., & Budhathoki, T. (2018). Conceptualising a digital orientation: Antecedents of supporting SME performance in the digital economy. *Journal of Strategic Marketing, 26*(5), 427–439.

Renko, M., Carsrud, A., & Brännback, M. (2009). The effect of a market orientation, entrepreneurial orientation, and technological capability on innovativeness: A study of young biotechnology ventures in the United States and in Scandinavia. *Journal of Small Business Management, 47*(3), 331–369.

Schweiger, S. A., Stettler, T. R., Baldauf, A., & Zamudio, C. (2019). The complementarity of strategic orientations: A meta-analytic synthesis and theory extension. *Strategic Management Journal, 40*(11), 1822–1851.

Sinkula, J. M., Baker, W. E., & Noordewier, T. (1997). A framework for market-based organizational learning: Linking values, knowledge, and behavior. *Journal of the Academy of Marketing Science, 25*(4), 305–318.

Sorescu, A., Frambach, R. T., Singh, J., Rangaswamy, A., & Bridges, C. (2011). Innovations in retail business models. *Journal of Retailing, 87*, 3–16.

Theodosiou, M., Kehagias, J., & Katsikea, E. (2012). Strategic orientations, marketing capabilities and firm performance: An empirical investigation in the context of frontline managers in service organizations. *Industrial Marketing Management, 41*(7), 1058–1070.

Tikhomirov, V., Dneprovskaya, N., & Yankovskaya, E. (2015). Three dimensions of smart education. In V. L. Uskov, R. J. Howlett, & L. C. Jain (Eds.), *Smart education and smart e-learning* (pp. 47–56). Springer.

Tucci, C. L., Afuah, A., & Viscusi, G. (Eds.). (2018). *Creating and capturing value through crowdsourcing*. Oxford University Press.

Urbinati, A., Bogers, M., Chiesa, V., & Frattini, F. (2019). Creating and capturing value from big data: A multiple-case study analysis of provider companies. *Technovation, 84*, 21–36.

Venkatraman, M. P. (1989). Opinion leaders, adopters, and communicative adopters: A role analysis. *Psychology & Marketing, 6*(1), 51–68.

Xiao, Y., Chen, X., Li, W., Liu, B., & Fang, D. (2013, August). An immune theory based health monitoring and risk evaluation of earthen sites with Internet of Things. *2013 IEEE International Conference on Green Computing and Communications and IEEE Internet of Things and IEEE Cyber, Physical and Social Computing* (pp. 378–382), Beijing, China.

Yoo, Y., Henfridsson, O., & Lyytinen, K. (2010). Research commentary—The new organizing logic of digital innovation: An agenda for information systems research. *Information Systems Research, 21*(4), 724–735.

3 Crowdsourcing and What's Next?

Regina Lenart-Gansiniec

3.1 The Concept and Essence of Crowdsourcing

In business practice, crowdsourcing has become a mega-trend that drives innovation, cooperation in research, business and society. More and more organizations are using crowdsourcing because of the potential business value related to innovative problem solving. Crowdsourcing also allows its users for managing crises, expanding current activities and offerings of the organization, creating the image of the organization, improving communication with the environment and optimizing the costs of the organization's operations. It also enables access to knowledge and creativity resources and facilitates the acquisition of new content and data outside the organization.

Although crowdsourcing is increasingly getting interest of scientific research, there are many ambiguities in the literature that result from the proliferation of different research approaches and perspectives. The research to date in the area of crowdsourcing has focused, among others, on: recognizing crowdsourcing as a new emerging network learning paradigm (Albors et al., 2008), which emerged with the introduction of digital and network technologies. Other studies focused on assessing the importance of crowdsourcing for open innovation, problem solving, optimization of organizational costs and improvement of business processes.

Although crowdsourcing has increased in the last five years, some scholars say the reference to crowdsourcing can be found as early as in the 17th century: in 1714 the British government established the Longitude Prize of £20,000 for helping to identify straight lines and practical ways of determining the position of ships at sea. Another example is the announcement by Louis XVI of a competition in 1791 to develop a method of producing alkali. In 1795, the French government announced a competition to develop a cheap and effective method of storing large amounts of food. Again, the French government, at the end of the 19th century, awarded inventors for identifying a butter substitute that could be used by the armed forces. Another example of a crowdsourcing initiative is the invitation at the end of the 19th century to create an Oxford English dictionary.

DOI: 10.4324/9781003227175-4

Crowdsourcing was also used to create logos: in 1916, the peanut company Planters: announced a competition to develop a logotype, and in 1936 Toyota also invited a logotype to be designed. Government organizations also drew on the ideas of the public: in 1957, the Australian government organized a competition for the design of the Sydney Opera House.

Crowdsourcing has been known for a long time, but only the advent of the Internet and other communication technologies opened up many possibilities for this phenomenon (Afuah and Tucci, 2012). According to D. C. Brabham, crowdsourcing is not "old wine in new bottles". In his opinion, the examples from the 17th or 18th century are not examples of crowdsourcing. For the author, we can talk about crowdsourcing when the organization has a task to perform, while the online community does it voluntarily. The result of these activities brings mutual benefit for both parties (Brabham, 2013). The reason for its creation is the Web 2.0 era, in which technologies and new media form the basis for the participation and use of knowledge found in online communities.

The first work devoted to crowdsourcing appeared relatively recently – in 2006, thanks to the article by J. Howe entitled: "The Rise of Crowdsourcing". He defined crowdsourcing as "… the act of taking a job traditionally performed by a designated agent (usually an employee) and outsourcing it to an undefined, generally large group of people in the form of an open call" (Howe, 2006). Over time, the author extended this definition to include the application of open-source principles, not only in terms of software but also outsourcing tasks to the crowd, matching the talent and knowledge of the crowd to the needs of the organization (Howe, 2008). From that moment on, there was an increase in interest in the issue of crowdsourcing, however, in the literature, often idiosyncratic definitions appeared.

The continuator of J. Howe's concept is Brabham (2008). He proposed the first definition, after a series of numerous publications in 2008–2012, in his 2013 book "Crowdsourcing". He found that crowdsourcing is an online, distributed model for problem-solving and production, a tool for social participation, planning for governments, and a method of building shared resources or processing large amounts of them. It is also a deliberate combination of a bottom-up, open and creative process with top-down organizational goals.

In 2010–2011, there was a sharp increase in the number of publications devoted to crowdsourcing. At this stage, the researchers adopted various research perspectives, focusing on the characteristics of the crowd (Buecheler et al., 2010; Doan et al., 2011), tasks (Ipeirotis et al., 2010) and mechanisms motivating the crowd to act (Alonso & Baeza-Yates, 2011; Karzai, 2011; Kaufmann et al., 2011). In those years, a multitude of, often contradictory, approaches to crowdsourcing were observed.

In response to this problem, in 2012, after analysing 40 definitions of crowdsourcing, a definition was proposed that aimed at integrating all previous attempts at definition. E. Estellés-Arolas and F. González-Ladrón-de-Guevara, based on an analysis of 209 publications from 2006–2011, proposed their definition. They considered crowdsourcing as "a type of participative online activity in which an individual, an institution, a non-profit organization, or company proposes to a group of individuals of varying knowledge, heterogeneity and number, via a flexible open call, the voluntary undertaking of a task. The undertaking of the task, of variable complexity and modularity, and in which the crowd should participate bringing their work, money, knowledge and/or experience, always entails mutual benefit. The user will receive their satisfaction of a given type of need, be it economic, social recognition, self-esteem, or the development of individual skills, while the crowdsourcer will obtain and utilize to their advantage that what the user has brought to the venture, whose form will depend on the type of activity undertaken" (Estellés-Arolas & González-Ladrón-de-Guevara, 2012, pp. 9–10). The definition proposed by the authors is often cited in the literature, but due to its extensiveness and high degree of complexity, it may reduce its practical value. Many authors refer to the features proposed by Estellés-Arolas and González-Ladrón-de-Guevara (2012), simplifying them and adapting them to the needs of their own research. For example, some authors emphasize the importance of software (Fitzgerald & Stol, 2014) and platforms (Zogaj et al., 2014), while others focus on the possibilities of the crowd (Xu et al., 2015). These adaptations indicate that there is a scarcity of a universal definition that could be applied to a variety of research and contexts.

Currently, both by theorists and practitioners, the term crowdsourcing is defined and understood in various ways. Despite the proliferation of considerations on crowdsourcing, the literature does not agree on the definition of crowdsourcing. It is interpreted not only as a way of solving problems (Brabham, 2008; Doan et al., 2011) or a method of collecting ideas (Kleeman et al., 2008) but also as a term accompanying all manifestations of Web 2.0 technology (Andriole, 2010). The literature indicates that crowdsourcing is a difficult concept, often vague, capacious and complex (Estellés-Arolas & González-Ladrón-de-Guevara, 2012), moreover, there are talks about the possibility of setting a conceptualization framework, common features or components of crowdsourcing (Vukovic & Bartolini, 2010). Sivula and Kantola (2015) aptly captured the issue of defining crowdsourcing, recognizing that it includes a human element, which therefore constitutes a challenge for researchers. Therefore, crowdsourcing can be considered a social phenomenon, and therefore one that exists thanks to the activities of the social community (Cacciattolo, 2015). As Gummesson (1993) points out, social phenomena are not precise. In addition, there is also a lack of consensus among researchers and a certain semantic confusion. Many terms such as open innovation, outsourcing and open resources are often used interchangeably. Nevertheless, in the field of management science, crowdsourcing is recognized as an important, highly current, interesting, but relatively new, poorly structured area of scientific inquiry. There is even a belief that crowdsourcing is an exciting new area of research (Lee, 2016), which in the years to come will be a dynamic and lively research area (Zhao & Zhu, 2014).

3.2 Components of Crowdsourcing

It should be emphasized that most authors agree that crowdsourcing is a complex concept (Brabham, 2008). However, a variety of components are listed that emphasize the flat and unsharp nature of the concept. Additionally, crowdsourcing is sometimes defined by distinguishing its components. It should be noted that the authors use similar names to denote the crowdsourcing components but indicate a different number of them. There was no consensus on this aspect. Estellés-Arolas and González-Ladrón-de Guevara (2012) attempted to put the above in order. Based on the analysis of 40 definitions of crowdsourcing from 2006 to 2011, the authors identified three components of crowdsourcing, i.e., crowd, initiator and process. This approach contrasts with the proposal of Aris (2017), who identified six components: user, process, task, platform, content and reward. In turn, Lars (2013), on the basis of a systematic review of the literature and an analysis of 17 definitions of crowdsourcing, distinguished four components: user management, task management, contribution management and workflow management. The four-element approach can also be found in works by other authors. Hosseini et al. (2015) propose the following components: crowd, crowdsourcer, task and platform. Among many studies, the three components of crowdsourcing are the most commonly identified. Zhao and Zhu (2014), based on a literature review, identified three components: participant, organization and system. The approach already cited above by E. Estellés-Arolas and F. González-Ladrón-de Guevara is conceptually close. Similar components of crowdsourcing are proposed by M. Kowalska, namely: the initiator, the crowd and the platform. A similar approach can be found in Geiger (2016), who suggests three components: participants, information and technology. Nevertheless, the component related to information is related to the transformation of existing information and the creation of new information as part of crowdsourcing. In turn, Fuchs-Kittowski and Faust (2014) identify three components: participant, campaign organizer and end user & participant. In this case, the end participant accesses and processes the data captured from the participants. When considering the authors' suggestions in the area of identifying the components of crowdsourcing, some similarities can be identified. The analysis of the literature shows three most commonly used components of crowdsourcing (crowd, initiator and technology). However, they may differ in terms of nomenclature. In some cases, the third component, technology, is sometimes referred to as a process (Estellés-Arolas & González-Ladrón-De-Guevara, 2012) or a system.

In one case (Aris & Din, 2016), it was divided into several smaller ones: content and reward. However, the authors do not indicate which of the listed components is central. Each of them is recognized equally.

As it has already been emphasized, crowdsourcing generally comes down to three components: crowd, initiator and technology. They are considered to be a kind of sine qua non condition. It is assumed that the basic building block of crowdsourcing is the wisdom of the crowd (Surowiecki, 2004). It is worth adding that a crowd is a community that shows a will to react and engage. It becomes a kind of virtual community. It is recognized that a group can achieve more benefits than any expert (Jeppesen & Lakhani, 2010; Leimeister, 2012).

Crowd is another important, if not the most important, element of crowdsourcing, referred to in the literature as the "virtual community". In the literature, next to this concept, the term "Internet community" is also used. These terms are often used interchangeably. What is more, there are no clearly defined differences between them (Inglis, 2013). Moreover, H. Rheingold (Lenart-Gansiniec, 2016) alternately uses the terms "virtual community" and "online community". Nevertheless, authors use the term "virtual community" more often in the literature.

Most authors recognize that crowd is diverse, heterogeneous and undefined in terms of knowledge and skills (Kleeman et al., 2008). It is a large community of people, a social network (Bloomfield 1997) that exceeds geographic, political and systemic limitations and performs voluntarily (Vecchia & Cisternino, 2010) in cyberspace specific tasks to achieve mutual interests and goals. More than once the concept of a crowd refers to the general Internet audience (Kleeman et al., 2008), a large group of people (Alonso & Lease, 2011; Howe, 2006; Poetz & Schreier, 2012; Sloane, 2011), people (Bederson & Quinn, 2011; Chanal & Caron-Fasan, 2008), crowd members (Kazai, 2011) who constitute users, consumers (Kleeman et al., 2008), customers (Porta et al., 2008), volunteers (Mazzola & Distefano, 2010), Internet community (Yang et al., 2008) or organized online communities (Whitla, 2009). They are identified as amateurs (usually students, school graduates), but also professionals and even scientists (Schenk & Guittard, 2011). For example, Jeppesen and Lakhani (2010), while studying the crowd around the InnoCentive platform, noticed that 65% of these people had a PhD degree. It is also debatable whether amateurs (Poetz & Schreier, 2012) can outperform professionals in the quality of crowdsourcing ideas generated. Certainly, crowdsourcing requires an intelligent and well-trained crowd (Howe, 2008). In addition, crowd members involved in crowdsourcing are often referred to as employees (Brabham, 2012; Mason & Suri, 2012), or network employees (Grier, 2010). In the literature, the authors involved propose a typology of crowds, taking into account their behaviour and contribution to the implementation of tasks. Vuurens and De Vries (2012) divide the crowd into: hardworking workers, sloppy workers, random spammers and patchy spammers. Based on the principle of inequality on the Internet, it is recognized that crowd members can be divided into: super contributors (1%) who provide the most contributions, associates (66%) who provide knowledge, but rarely participate actively in tasks (33%). Another division points to lookers, users, those who are aspiring and those who are communal (Martineau, 2012). Kazai et al. (2011) found that members of the crowd may perform tasks dishonestly, randomly and inaccurately.

The role of the crowd, thanks to the accumulation of knowledge and skills, is to voluntarily perform tasks, solve problems or undertake any activity (Jain, 2010). The basis of their activities is interacting and building relationships (Hsu et al., 2007). It is recognized that a group can achieve and work out more benefits than any expert (Leimeister, 2012). The literature indicates that members of the virtual community joining crowdsourcing have different motives.

Among the reasons for building and forming virtual communities in literature, the following are indicated:

1 a sense of connection with other members of the community;
2 communicating with people with similar interests;
3 the need for constant access to information and knowledge;
4 the opportunity to participate in games, gameplay;
5 the possibility of being anonymous, changing identity;
6 the ability to conduct commercial transactions;
7 providing knowledge, especially readiness to share knowledge with other participants (Chiu et al., 2006)

Often times, the need for satisfaction, building one's own reputation and the will to have fun (Stewart et al., 2009) are more important than financial motivation (Kazai, 2011).

The initiator in crowdsourcing is referred to in the literature as a crowdsourcer, i.e., a person or people who can mobilize a potentially useful crowd to act (Franke et al., 2006; Jeppesen & Laursen, 2009). Most authors believe that the crowdsourcer is an organization (Vecchia & Cisternino, 2010). Only a few authors recognize that the initiator does not always have to be a commercial organization – it may be a governmental or non-profit institution (Brabham, 2008). Thus, an initiator can be any entity that has the financial resources to start a crowdsourcing initiative. This means that crowdsourcing is not only a business model for companies but also a problem-solving tool for the government or non-profit sectors.

Most authors agree that the initiator joining crowdsourcing wants to maximize the assumed benefits of a given task (Vukovic, 2009). As already mentioned, the role of the initiator is to send an open invitation to cooperation to the crowd via the crowdsourcing platform and to define the tasks to be solved. It is important here that the initiator determines the goal, scope, schedule, expectations, rewards or the group of recipients. The initiator should also, during the project duration, control its course, e.g., evaluate the incoming ideas/solutions, answer participants' questions. Tasks are the basic elements of crowdsourcing that define organizations and communicate them to members of the crowd for execution (Aris & Din, 2016; Whitla, 2009). Few authors treat them as a separate component of crowdsourcing. However, due to the fact that the crowdsourcer should specify, inter alia, the scope of the project (Rosen, 2011) it was assumed that this component may be included in the organizational factor. This approach will also be adopted in this work.

According to Vakkari (2003), a task can be defined as an abstract description of the work content or an illustration of a work process that can be divided and combined. This definition has further consequences: researchers often focused on the characteristics or functions of the task itself and its characteristics (Nevo et al., 2012; Ye & Kankanhalli, 2013) and attributes (Shao et al., 2012), behaviours or actions related to tasks to complete a specific task, task design (Alagarai Sampath et al., 2014), task assignments (Ho & Vaughan, 2012; Jiang & Matsubara, 2014; Kulkarni et al., 2012) or performance evaluation (Nickerson et al., 2012; Rogstadius et al., 2011). In addition, some researchers try to qualify crowdsourcing projects by adopting a perspective that combines the attributes of tasks with their benefits (Geiger et al., 2012; Kaufmann et al., 2011). Zhao and Zhu (2012) suggest getting to know the complexity of tasks before the crowdsourcing initiative.

The crowdsourcing platform is another key element of crowdsourcing, recognized in the literature. It acts as a mediator between the organization and the crowd (Hirth et al., 2010). Generally speaking, its significance results from the benefits that an organization can obtain thanks to the use of a given technology (Duan et al., 2012), further the ability to capture explicit and hidden knowledge of the virtual community (Alt et al., 2010; Chatzimilioudis et al., 2012) and compatibility (Chong et al., 2009; Lee & Shim, 2007; MacKay et al., 2004).

The existing platforms may differ from each other in terms of technical capabilities, application, range of influence, purpose. For example, Vukovic (2009) describes the classification of existing crowdsourcing platforms and the technical requirements. The author takes into account two criteria of division: functionality and working mode. Functional platforms allow for the creation of innovations, development and testing, support for the activities of the organization – they are intended for marketing and sales activities. On the other hand, mode-oriented platforms may be intended for the organization of competitions or activities related to the performance of a task. Another division covers specialized platforms and those that focus on specific tasks (Hirth et al., 2011). Specialized platforms can be used to solve problems (Malone et al., 2010; Redi et al., 2013), while task platforms can support the organization in carrying out simple tasks, i.e., data collection, transcription or categorization.

3.3 Typology of Crowdsourcing

Crowdsourcing is a complex and multi-element concept (Estellés-Arolas et al., 2015). This diversity is due to the fact that crowdsourcing is not a homogeneous phenomenon. Its heterogeneity is additionally caused by the multiplicity of elements, processes, the multiplicity of tasks and the heterogeneity of the crowd (Zhang et al., 2015). Therefore, an important aspect is its typology, which combines the greatest information content with the simplest way to search for information and constitutes a conceptual classification system (Rich, 1992). It provides an effective way of organizing data and information, the search and development of theories, and enables the study of relationships (Nickerson et al., 2013). The literature indicates various types or typologies of crowdsourcing, which are largely based on the types of crowdsourcing initiatives. The most commonly used breakdowns are summarized in Table 3.1.

It can be concluded that the types of crowdsourcing identified above are characterized by quite a different degree of generality and complexity. Each of them takes into account different separation criteria. Thus, due to the objectives and specificity of this study, those aimed at acquiring knowledge, skills or competences from the crowd seem to be particularly important. As mentioned before, crowdsourcing is based on the wisdom of members of the online community – hence the resource-oriented types of crowdsourcing will be discussed in the following. There is some frequency of citing particular types of crowdsourcing and it is possible to observe that the authors often gave their names to define the same, for example Estellés-Arolas and González-Ladrón-de-Guevara (2012) referred to content creation as crowdcasting, while J. Howe – crowd creation, and D. C. Brabham – distributed human-intelligence tasking. Nevertheless, the two most frequently quoted divisions are those of J. Howe and D. C. Brabham.

3.3.1 Division by J. Howe

Wisdom of the crowd (another term for collective intelligence) is one of the types of crowdsourcing specified by J. Howe. It is understood as the solution of organizational problems by the crowd. In this perspective, the central point is that the group has more knowledge than the individual. This knowledge may turn out to be useful for an organization when it wants to solve a problem, predict certain events, certain activities or tasks. Howe (2008) calls this type of crowdsourcing a suggestion box and the idea jams form.

Crowd creation is another type of crowdsourcing specified by J. Howe. It concerns the use by the organization of the creative potential of crowd members to create new products, services and content. It also includes content generation and evaluation. This type of crowdsourcing is also known as crowd casting. It is the solution by a crowd of specific problems or the

Table 3.1 Typologies of crowdsourcing

Author/authors	Separation criteria	Types	Characteristic
Howe (2008)	Tasks for the crowd	Collective intelligence, wisdom of the crowd Crowd creation Crowd voting Crowdfunding	Problem solving by the crowd Creating new products Choosing the best solutions, collecting opinions Community fundraising
Kleeman et al. (2008)	Tasks for the crowd	Participation of consumers in product development and configuration Product design Competitive bids on specifically defined tasks or problems Permanent open calls Community reporting Product rating by consumers and consumer profiling Customer-to-customer support	Product development and configuration Product design Performing a specific task or solving a problem Gathering information Reporting information about the need for a new product or trend Product evaluation Solving other users' problems
Brabham	Problem to be solved	Knowledge discovery and management Broadcast search Peer-vetted creative production Distributed human-intelligence tasking	Information search and storage Looking for ideas on problems reported by the organization Creative co-creation, solving image, social and political problems Data processing or analysis
Vukovic (2009)	Platform capabilities	Crowdsourcer functions Platform mode	Design, development, testing, marketing and sales capabilities Market or competition concentration
Corney et al. (2009)	The specificity of the task	Creation, evaluation and organization A task for everyone, a task for specialists A voluntary task, a paid task	The nature of the task The nature of the crowd The nature of the payment

(Continued)

Table 3.1 Typologies of crowdsourcing (Continued)

Author/authors	Separation criteria	Types	Characteristic
Geerts (2009)	Tasks for the crowd	Prediction markets	Predictive markets
		Crowd casting	Competing for the prize by providing the best ideas to solve the problem
		Crowd creation	User-generated content
		Crowd voting	Expressing opinions by voting
		Idea jam	Brainstorming, trying to solve problems together
		Crowd storming	Discussing, asking questions, proposing alternative ways to solve the problem
		Crowd production	Development of a database, content, tagging of web resources
		Crowdfunding	Community fundraising
Corney et al. (2009)	Purpose of crowdsourcing	Task-based crowdsourcing	Intended for the implementation of evaluation and creative tasks related to the organization of content
		Engaging crowdsourcing	Designed for individuals, communities and experts
		Crowdsourcing related to return benefits	Volunteering, non-material rewards, financial and material rewards
Rouse (2010)	The complexity of the task	Simple, complicated and moderate	The nature of the task
		Individual, community oriented	Distribution of benefits
		Rewarding, altruistic, based on personal satisfaction and social status	Forms of motivation
Vukovic and Bartolini (2010)	Type of crowd	Internal	Use of employees' knowledge
		External	Use of the knowledge of Internet communities
Dawson (2010)	Tasks for the crowd	Content	Acquiring creative content
		Idea management	Generating new ideas
		Crowdfunding	Creating and financing new products
		Insight	Giving opinions
		Citizen engagement	Involvement in the life of the organization
		Word-of-mouth	Acting as a brand spokesperson

(Continued)

Table 3.1 Typologies of crowdsourcing (Continued)

Author/authors	Separation criteria	Types	Characteristic
Doan et al. (2011)	System requirements	The nature of cooperation, the type of target problem, methods of recruiting and engaging the crowd, tasks for the crowd, combining and evaluating crowd ideas, manual control, user division and architecture	System design
Burger-Helmchen and Pénin (2011)	Purpose	Crowdsourcing of routine activities Crowdsourcing of content Crowdsourcing of inventive activities	Crowdsourcing of routine tasks Crowdsourcing of content Crowdsourcing of inventive activities
Geiger et al. (2011)	Breakdown of processes	Initial crowd selection Modification, evaluation, review Aggregating access Salary for work	Based on qualifications Access to interconnection Integrative or selective approach Fixed remuneration based on winnings, none
Schenk and Guittard (2011)	The type of the process	Integrative, selective Simple, complex and creative	Nature of the process Nature of the task
Estellés-Arolas and González-Ladrón-de-Guevara (2012)	Tasks for the crowd	Crowd casting Crowd collaboration Crowd storming Crowd support Crowd content Crowd production Crowd searching Crowd analysing Crowdfunding Crowd opinion	Execution by the crowd of the task Common problem solving Submitting ideas to improve performance Support for other users Individual knowledge sharing Content creation Content search Analysing Fundraising for project financing Sending feedback on a given topic
Geiger (2016)	Tasks for the crowd	Crowd processing Crowd rating Crowd solving Crowd creation	Data processing Voting and evaluating Sending ready-made, optimal solutions and ideas for organizational problems Collective production, generation and aggregation of knowledge

Source: Own study.

performance of specific tasks, for which the crowd receive certain rewards. The winner is the one who sends the solutions first or best. This type of crowdsourcing focuses mainly on individual, but creative work. The crowd collaboration is similar to this – the crowd is also involved in solving problems. However, they do not receive financial rewards for their activity, and the motivation is internal satisfaction. E. Estellés-Arolas distinguishes two crowd collaboration sub-types, i.e., crowd storming and crowd support. In crowd storming, the crowd is looking for ideas to improve organizational performance, products or services. However, in the case of crowd support, the crowd is involved in solving the problems of many organizations at the same time. This usually happens within a platform where many organizations post their requests to the online community. The crowd content (sub-types: crowd production, crowd searching, crowd analysing) indicated by E. Estellés-Arolas also focuses on creating content. Crowd members work individually to create different types of content, such as: translating texts, images (crowd production), searching the Internet for a specific purpose (crowd searching) or analysing images or videos (crowd analysing). The results of the work of individual members of the Internet community are combined, and only the whole thing gains value.

Crowd voting is a situation in which members of the Internet community are tasked with gathering opinions, judgments, and choosing the best solutions – often among the propositions submitted by other members of the crowd. The crowd may also filter and rank different online content. Providing feedback, rating and reviewing was also specified by E. Estellés-Arolas and referred to as crowd opinion. However, the author points out here that this type of crowdsourcing does not involve voting.

Crowdfunding has already been partially discussed in this study. Nevertheless, according to J. Howe's approach – it concerns community fundraising for various purposes and activities of the organization. The author describes it as a collective pocketbook, where the crowd becomes a kind of bank. Some of the authors separate crowdfunding and omit it in crowdsourcing typologies (Kazmark, 2013), but J. Howe considers it to be one of the types of crowdsourcing.

3.3.2 Division by D. C. Brabham

The division proposed by D. C. Brabham focuses on the issue of problem solving. Therefore, he distinguished four types of crowdsourcing. Knowledge discovery and management gives the crowd the task of searching and storing information in a specific place, which will allow the organization to allocate resources or make better decisions. In addition, online communities can report emerging problems, such as holes in the road, blocked storm sewers, broken traffic lights, holes in the asphalt or graffiti – then crowdsourcing becomes an online civic communication channel (Brabham, 2013).

Broadcast search is the search for ideas, solutions and answers to the usually difficult, scientific or empirical problems reported by the organization, or the creation of innovative solutions, changes in legal regulations or technologies.

Peer-vetted creative production is generating new ideas by users, testing products or services, solving image, design, social and political problems, i.e., those that require a subjective point of view. Additionally, members of the Internet community are encouraged by the organization to comment, vote or generate new designs for existing products or services.

Distributed human-intelligence tasking is the processing of large amounts of data by members of the Internet community, information management, finding and collecting it, transcription of records and translation of documents. These are tasks that often cannot be dealt with by advanced computer systems.

Another division refers to external and internal crowdsourcing. The former is based on the use of knowledge found in online communities, while the internal one is based on encouraging the cooperation of employees of your own organization. Due to the fact that this division is omitted in the literature, a comparison of both types is presented below. It is also emphasized that the work focuses solely on external crowdsourcing. This is due to the goal of the work – internal crowdsourcing is suggested for large organizations with numerous branches located all over the world (Byrén, 2013).

In the context of universities, separate types of crowdsourcing have also been distinguished in the literature. For example, Llorente and Morant (2015) indicate four types of crowdsourcing, such as: crowd teaching, crowd learning, crowd tuition and crowdfunding.

1   Crowd teaching: in this approach, lecturers share and put together lecture material in line with the curricula.
2   Crowd learning: learning through the design lectures pattern. The knowledge building process is based on collaborative projects where students share, learn from each other effectively and together learn the skills that are essential to achieving the project's goals.
3   Crowd tuition: resembles a grant. Students may obtain a loan that can be used to cover tuition fees. The aim is to ensure that the knowledge and skills acquired by students at a university are transferred back to that institution through the recruitment of graduates upon completion of their PhDs.
4   Crowdfunding: acquiring funds for various university activities, from equipping laboratories to co-financing a sports team, to building university infrastructure.

It is also postulated in the literature that crowdsourcing can be used for vocational training of educational managers (Makhynia, 2018). In this approach, the use of crowdsourcing in managerial education will provide students and faculty with access to a wider educational community of practitioners. In particular, students and student groups can directly participate in online message boards and share work with business practitioners. This is particularly important as business schools are under increasing pressure from practitioners, the wider community and students to offer profitable study programmes (Jackson, 2012).

3.4 Crowdsourcing Trends

The literature review shows that the increased interest in crowdsourcing may result from its potential, but also from the dynamic development of ICT technologies. Firstly, crowdsourcing at an appropriate level favours solving organizational problems (Brabham, 2008). For example, it may determine the involvement of members of the Internet community – in particular, it is valuable to diversify them, especially in terms of knowledge. Through conscious involvement of the Internet community, their willingness to cooperate with the organization, but often knowledge of its specifics, it will be able to obtain unique, creative solutions or projects (Terwiesch & Xu, 2008), often with a lower financial outlay and in a shorter time (Hosseini et al., 2014). Crowdsourcing is therefore conducive to communication and cooperation on a specific task to be performed (Brabham, 2012).

Secondly, crowdsourcing enables and facilitates establishing and building relationships and cooperation with online communities (Albors et al., 2008), which in turn favours the transfer of external knowledge, talents (Burger-Helmchen & Pénin, 2010) and valuable information (Greengard, 2011), skills and experience (Oliveira et al., 2010), competences (Chanal & Caron-Fasan, 2008). This stimulates organizational learning and the organization's openness to new external knowledge (Feller et al., 2012; Majchrzak & Malhotra, 2013). In addition, crowdsourcing enables crowd capital to be shaped. It is a side effect that arises when the knowledge, talent and competences of the crowd are combined with intra-organizational structures and processes (Lenart-Gansiniec, 2016).

To sum up, it can be said that the role of crowdsourcing for organizations is dynamic, which is reflected in the multitude of its potential. This leads to an increase in the level of innovation, general civilization and technological progress – for the supporters it has become a kind of panacea for all organizational problems.

The scientific achievements to date indicate that the appropriate level of crowdsourcing allows access to the resources of human knowledge and creativity outside the organization, facilitates the acquisition of new ideas, content, information, ideas to solve problems, while reducing financial outlays and time. Additionally, it creates opportunities for access to global labour markets and cheaper labour. Thanks to crowdsourcing, the organization, having feedback from the crowd, can better adapt its offer to the needs of direct users, which leads to increased efficiency, productivity, competitiveness and innovation. It should also be emphasized that the issue of refreshing or building the image of the organization is the one that is creative and open to customers, extending the current activity and obtaining additional funds. Thanks to crowdsourcing, the organization can create and maintain contacts with Internet communities interested in co-creation.

In a broader sense, it can be said that crowdsourcing is a mechanism and means for coordinating and cooperating with the crowd. Crowdsourcing is perceived by the authors as a new component of knowledge. It can have a positive impact on employee learning (Deng & Chandler, 2010) and building a learning organization. It enables better acquisition of new, not once dispersed knowledge, increases the transfer, sharing and diffusion of knowledge, and transforms it into innovation. It can also be stated that it not only positively influences various processes but also improves knowledge management (Callaghan, 2016). It becomes the key to obtaining value from external knowledge (Rajala et al., 2013). From this perspective, crowdsourcing can contribute to organizational learning.

In addition to many advantages, it is important to remember that possibilities of using crowdsourcing are changing and crowdsourcing becomes valuable not only in the context of access to knowledge or the experience of the crowd.

Firstly, crowdsourcing as a new way to do a variety of things involves various aspects such as crowdfunding, co-creation, collaboration and open innovation. In this sense, crowdsourcing provides the opportunity to rethink and re-invent conventional processes with far more innovations. It is recognized as a new innovation model (https://hbr.org/2020/01/a-new-model-for-crowdsourcing-innovation).

Secondly, crowdsourcing is becoming increasingly recognized as one of the innovative tools for higher education development (Saleh & Julia, 2019). There is some conviction among crowdsourcing promoters in higher education institutions that it can be useful for gaining ideas, opinions, feedback from the virtual community, gaining support for various projects, as well as improving communication between individual stakeholders, and even collecting data as part of scientific research, creating textbooks and raising funds for educational projects. In the case of the latter, it is indicated that the use of crowdsourcing allows for the optimization of the institution's budget and a more effective use of time for study (Llorente & Morant, 2015).

Thirdly, the latest trend in the context of crowdsourcing refers to the need to develop management mechanisms. It should be emphasized that the use of crowdsourcing may entail threats. Crowdsourcing is not a panacea for all the problems of the organization. As P. Dutil points out, crowdsourcing will not replace the state. According to her, crowdsourcing is "an instrument, a choice that the state must consider in pursuing its goals" (Dutil, 2015, p. 380). Poorly managed crowdsourcing can make the virtual community dissatisfied with the mere participation in the crowdsourcing initiative, which can contribute to discouragement and dissatisfaction and negative perception of the initiator. Crowdsourcing may generate excessive costs while reducing the performance of members of the virtual community in relation to that of experts. The organization may obtain low-quality solutions. Bryer and Cooper (2012) note that the cost of engaging a virtual community can drain resources from professional administrative work. Crowdsourcing may limit innovation because creating ideas takes time, and crowdsourcing focuses on speed (Majchrzak & Malhotra, 2013).

According to the researchers, group creativity requires that colleagues know each other, and members of virtual communities usually do not know each other. Another limitation concerns the knowledge of the specificity of a given issue. For example, I. Mergel and her colleagues analysed 203 projects posted on the Challenge.gov platform and concluded that most of them were about information and education campaigns that help them better understand how to improve service delivery (Mergel et al., 2014). Despite the risks and limitations, the use of crowdsourcing in higher education can increase the efficiency of learning processes and optimize curricula, which can lead to better student outcomes.

References

Afuah, A., & Tucci, C. L. (2012). Crowdsourcing as a solution to distant search. *Academy of Management Review, 37*(3), 355–375.

Alagarai Sampath, H., Rajeshuni, R., & Indurkhya, B. (2014). Cognitively inspired task design to improve user performance on crowdsourcing platforms. In Proceedings of the SIGCHI Conference on Human Factors in Computing Systems (CHI '14). Association for Computing Machinery, New York, NY, USA, 3665–3674. https://doi.org/10.1145/2556288.2557155.

Albors, J., Ramos, J. C., & Hervas, J. L. (2008). New learning network paradigms: Communities of objectives, crowdsourcing, wikis and open source. *International Journal of Information Management, 28*(3), 194–202.

Albors, J., Ramos, J. C., & Hervas, J. L. (2008). New learning network paradigms: Communities of objectives, crowdsourcing, wikis and open source. *International Journal of Information Management, 28*(3), 194–202.

Alonso, O., & Baeza-Yates, R. (2011). Design and implementation of relevance assessments using crowdsourcing. *European Conference on Information Retrieval* (pp. 153–164), Berlin, Heidelberg.

Alonso, O., & Lease, M. (2011). Crowdsourcing 101: Putting the WSDM of crowds to work for you. *Proceedings of the Fourth ACM International Conference on Web Search and Data Mining*, Hong Kong.

Alt, F., Shirazi, A. S., Schmidt, A., Kramer, U., & Nawaz, Z. (2010, October). Location-based crowdsourcing: extending crowdsourcing to the real world. *Proceedings of the 6th Nordic Conference on Human-Computer Interaction: Extending Boundaries* (pp. 13–22), Reykjavik, Iceland.

Andriole, S. J. (2010). Business impact of web 2.0 technologies. *Communications of the ACM*, *53*(12), 67–79.

Aris, H. (2017, April). Current state of crowdsourcing taxonomy research: A systematic review. *Proceedings of the 6th International Conference on Computing and Informatics* (Vol. 259, p. 260), Kuala Lumpur, Malaysia.

Aris, H., & Din, M. M. (2016, March). Crowdsourcing evolution: Towards a taxonomy of crowdsourcing initiatives. *2016 IEEE International Conference on Pervasive Computing and Communication Workshops* (pp. 1–6), Sydney, NSW, Australia.

Bederson, B. B., & Quinn, A. J. (2011). Web workers unite! addressing challenges of online laborers *Extended Abstracts on Human Factors in Computing Systems* (pp. 97–106), Vancouver, BC, Canada.

Brabham, D. C. (2008). Crowdsourcing as a model for problem solving: An introduction and cases. *Convergence*, *14*(1), 75–90.

Brabham, D. C. (2012). Motivations for participation in a crowdsourcing application to improve public engagement in transit planning. *Journal of Applied Communication Research*, *40*(3), 307–328.

Brabham, D. C. (2013). *Crowdsourcing*. MIT Press.

Bryer, T. A., & Cooper, T. L. (2012). H. George Frederickson and the dialogue on citizenship in public administration. *Public Administration Review*, *72*(s1), S108–S116.

Buecheler, T., Sieg, J. H., Füchslin, R. M., & Pfeifer, R. (2010, August 19–23). Crowdsourcing, open innovation and collective intelligence in the scientific method: A research agenda and operational framework. *The 12th International Conference on the Synthesis and Simulation of Living Systems* (pp. 679–686), Odense, Denmark.

Burger-Helmchen, T., & Pénin, J. (2010, March). The limits of crowdsourcing inventive activities: What do transaction cost theory and the evolutionary theories of the firm teach us. *Workshop on Open Source Innovation* (pp. 1–26), Strasbourg, France.

Burger-Helmchen, T., & Pénin, J. (2011). Crowdsourcing: Définition, enjeux, typologie. *Management Avenir*, (1), 254–269.

Byrén, E. (2013). *Internal crowdsourcing for innovation development: How multi-national companies can obtain the advantages of crowdsourcing utilising internal resources* [Master's thesis], Chalmers University of Technology, Gothenburg, Sweden.

Cacciattolo, K. (2015). Defining organisational communication. *European Scientific Journal*, *11*(20), 79–87.

Callaghan, C. W. (2016). A new paradigm of knowledge management: Crowdsourcing as emergent research and development. *Southern African Business Review*, *20*(1), 1–28.

Chanal, V., & Caron-Fasan, M. L. (2008, May). How to invent a new business model based on crowdsourcing: The Crowdspirit® case. *Conférence de l'Association Internationale de Management Stratégique* (pp. 1–27), Nice, France.

Chatzimilioudis, G., Konstantinidis, A., Laoudias, C., & Zeinalipour-Yazti, D. (2012). Crowdsourcing with smartphones. *IEEE Internet Computing*, *16*(5), 36–44.

Chiu, C. M., Hsu, M. H., & Wang, E. T. (2006). Understanding knowledge sharing in virtual communities: An integration of social capital and social cognitive theories. *Decision Support Systems*, *42*(3), 1872–1888.

Chong, A. Y. L., Lin, B., Ooi, K. B., & Raman, M. (2009). Factors affecting the adoption level of c-commerce: An empirical study. *Journal of Computer Information Systems*, *50*(2), 13–22.

Corney, J. R., Torres-Sánchez, C., Jagadeesan, A. P., & Regli, W. C. (2009). Outsourcing labour to the cloud. *International Journal of Innovation and Sustainable Development*, 4(4), 294–313.

Corney, J. R., Torres-Sanchez, C., Jagadeesan, A. P., Yan, X. T., Regli, W. C., & Medellin, H. (2010). Putting the crowd to work in a knowledge-based factory. *Advanced Engineering Informatics*, 24(3), 243–250.

Dawson, R. (2010). Six tools to kickstart your crowdsourcing strategy. MyCustomer. https://www.mycustomer.com/marketing/strategy/ross-dawson-six-tools-to-kickstart-your-crowdsourcing-strategy

Deng, X. N., & Chandler, J., (2010). Learning in enterprise system support: Specialization, task type and network characteristics. *Proceedings of the International Conference on Information Systems*, Saint Louis, MI.

Doan, A., Ramakrishnan, R., & Halevy, A. Y. (2011). Crowdsourcing systems on the world-wide web. *Communications of the ACM*, 54(4), 86–96.

Duan, X., Deng, H., & Corbitt, B. (2012). Evaluating the critical determinants for adopting e-market in Australian small-and-medium sized enterprises. *Management Research Review*, 35(3/4), 289–308.

Dutil, P. (2015). Crowdsourcing as a new instrument in the government's arsenal: Explorations and considerations. *Canadian Public Administration*, 58(3), 363–383.

Estellés-Arolas, E., & González-Ladrón-de-Guevara, F. (2012). Towards an integrated crowdsourcing definition. *Journal of Information Science*, 38(2), 189–200.

Estellés-Arolas, E., Navarro-Giner, R., & González-Ladrón-de-Guevara, F. (2015). Crowdsourcing fundamentals: Definition and typology. In F. J. Garrigos-Simon, I. Gil-Pechuán, & S. Estelles-Miguel (Eds.), *Advances in crowdsourcing* (pp. 33–48). Springer.

Feller, J., Finnegan, P., Hayes, J., & O'Reilly, P. (2012). 'Orchestrating' sustainable crowdsourcing: A characterisation of solver brokerages. *The Journal of Strategic Information Systems*, 21(3), 216–232.

Fitzgerald, B., & Stol, K. J. (2014, June). Continuous software engineering and beyond: Trends and challenges. *Proceedings of the 1st International Workshop on Rapid Continuous Software Engineering* (pp. 1–9), Hyderabad, India.

Franke, N., Von Hippel, E., & Schreier, M. (2006). Finding commercially attractive user innovations: A test of lead-user theory. *Journal of Product Innovation Management*, 23(4), 301–315.

Fuchs-Kittowski, F., & Faust, D. (2014, September). Architecture of mobile crowdsourcing systems. In N. Baloian, F. Burstein, H. Ogata, F. Santoro, & G. Zurita (Eds.), *CYTED-RITOS international workshop on groupware* (pp. 121–136). Springer.

Geerts, S. (2009). *Discovering crowdsourcing: theory, classification and directions for use*. [Unpublished Master's thesis], Eindhoven University of Technology.

Geiger, D. (2016). Crowdsourcing systems. In *Personalized task recommendation in crowdsourcing systems* (pp. 7–14). Springer.

Geiger, D., Rosemann, M., & Fielt, E. (2011). Crowdsourcing information systems–A systems theory perspective. *Proceedings of the Australasian Conference on Information Systems*, Washington, DC.

Geiger, D., Rosemann, M., Fielt, E., & Schader, M. (2012). Crowdsourcing information systems – Definition, typology, and design. In J. F. George (Ed.), *Proceedings of the 33rd annual international conference on information system*. AIS Electronic Library.

Greengard, S. (2011). Following the crowd. *Communications of the ACM*, 54(2), 20–22.

Gummesson, E. (1993). *Quality Management in Service Organization*. New York: International Service Quality Association.

Howe, J. (2008). *Crowdsourcing: How the power of the crowd is driving the future of business*. Random House.

Hirth, M., Hoßfeld, T., & Tran-Gia, P. (2010). Cheat-detection mechanisms for crowdsourcing (*Technical Report, 4*). University of Würzburg.

Hirth, M., Hoßfeld, T., & Tran-Gia, P. (2011, June). Anatomy of a crowdsourcing platform-using the example of microworkers.com. *2011 Fifth International Conference on Innovative Mobile and Internet Services in Ubiquitous Computing* (pp. 322–329), Seoul, South Korea.

Ho, C. J., & Vaughan, J. (2012). Online task assignment in crowdsourcing markets. *Proceedings of the AAAI Conference on Artificial Intelligence* (Vol. 26, No. 1, pp. 45–51), Toronto, Ontario, Canada.

Hosseini, M., Phalp, K., Taylor, J., & Ali, R. (2014, May). The four pillars of crowdsourcing: A reference model. *2014 IEEE Eighth International Conference on Research Challenges in Information Science* (pp. 1–12). Marrakech, Morocco.

Hosseini, M., Shahri, A., Phalp, K., Taylor, J., & Ali, R. (2015). Crowdsourcing: A taxonomy and systematic mapping study. *Computer Science Review, 17*, 43–69.

Howe, J. (2006). The rise of crowdsourcing. *Wired Magazine, 14*(6), 1–4.

Hsu, M. H., Ju, T. L., Yen, C. H., & Chang, C. M. (2007). Knowledge sharing behavior in virtual communities: The relationship between trust, self-efficacy, and outcome expectations. *International Journal of Human-Computer Studies, 65*(2), 153–169.

Ipeirotis, P. G., Provost, F., & Wang, J. (2010, July). Quality management on Amazon mechanical turk. *Proceedings of the ACM SIGKDD Workshop on Human Computation* (pp. 64–67), Washington, DC.

Jackson, D. (2012). An international profile of industry-relevant competencies and skill gaps in modern graduates. *International Journal of Management Education, 10*(2), 29–58.

Jain, R. (2010). Investigation of governance mechanisms for crowdsourcing initiatives. *16th Americas Conference on Information Systems*, Lima, Peru.

Jeppesen, L. B., & Lakhani, K. R. (2010). Marginality and problem-solving effectiveness in broadcast search. *Organization Science, 21*(5), 1016–1033.

Jeppesen, L. B., & Laursen, K. (2009). The role of lead users in knowledge sharing. *Research Policy, 38*(10), 1582–1589.

Jiang, H., & Matsubara, S. (2014, December). Efficient task decomposition in crowdsourcing. In B. An, A. Bazzan, J. Leite, S. Villata, & L. van der Torre (Eds.), *International conference on principles and practice of multi-agent systems* (pp. 65–73). Springer.

Kaufmann, N., Schulze, T., & Veit, D. (2011). More than fun and money. Worker motivation in crowdsourcing – A study on mechanical turk. *Americas Conference on Information Systems*, Detroit, MI.

Kazai, G. (2011, April). In search of quality in crowdsourcing for search engine evaluation. In *European Conference on information retrieval* (pp. 165–176). Springer.

Kazai, G., Kamps, J., & Milic-Frayling, N. (2011, October). Worker types and personality traits in crowdsourcing relevance labels. *Proceedings of the 20th ACM International Conference on Information and Knowledge Management* (pp. 1941–1944), Glasgow, UK.

Kazmark, Justin. (2013). Kickstarter before Kickstarter. *Kickstarter*. July 18, 2013, https:// www.kickstarter.com/blog/kickstarter-before-kickstarter

Kleeman, F., Voss, G., & Rieder, K. (2008). Un (der) paid innovators: The commercial utilization of consumer work through crowdsourcing. *Science, Technology & Innovation Studies*, *4*(1), 5–26.

Kulkarni, A., Can, M., & Hartmann, B. (2012, February). Collaboratively crowdsourcing workflows with turkomatic. *Proceedings of the ACM 2012 Conference on Computer Supported Cooperative Work* (pp. 1003–1012), Seattle, WA.

Lee, H. (2016). Collective intelligence-based idea platform with linked data. *2016 International Conference on Big Data and Smart Computing (BigComp)*, 521–524. doi: 10.1109/BIGCOMP.2016.7425984

Lee, C. P., & Shim, J. P. (2007). An exploratory study of radio frequency identification (RFID) adoption in the healthcare industry. *European Journal of Information Systems*, *16*(6), 712–724.

Leimeister, J. M. (2012). Crowdsourcing. *Controlling & Management*, *56*(6), 388–392.

Lenart-Gansiniec, R. (2016). Crowd capital–conceptualisation attempt. *International Journal of Contemporary Management*, *15*(2), 29–57.

Llorente, R., & Morant, M. (2015). Crowdsourcing in higher education. In F. J. Garrigos-Simon, I. Gil-Pechuán, & S. Estelles-Miguel (Eds.), *Advances in crowdsourcing* (pp. 87–95). Springer.

MacKay, N., Parent, M., & Gemino, A. (2004). A model of electronic commerce adoption by small voluntary organizations. *European Journal of Information Systems*, *13*(2), 147–159.

Majchrzak, A., & Malhotra, A. (2013). Towards an information systems perspective and research agenda on crowdsourcing for innovation. *The Journal of Strategic Information Systems*, *22*(4), 257–268.

Makhynia, T. (2018). Possibility of crowdsourcing usage in professional training of education managers. *Kultura–Przemiany–Edukacja*, *6*, 268–277.

Malone, T. W., Laubacher, R., & Dellarocas, C. (2010). The collective intelligence genome. *MIT Sloan Management Review*, *51*(3), 21.

Martineau, E. (2012). A typology of crowdsourcing participation styles [Doctoral dissertation], Concordia University, Montreal, QC, Canada.

Mason, W., & Suri, S. (2012). Conducting behavioral research on Amazon's mechanical Turk. *Behavior Research Methods*, *44*(1), 1–23.

Mazzola, D., & Distefano, A. (2010, October). Crowdsourcing and the participation process for problem solving: The case of BP. *Proceedings of ItAIS 2010 VII Conference of the Italian Chapter of AIS* (pp. 42–49), Napoles, Italy.

Mergel, I., Bretschneider, S. I., Louis, C., & Smith, J. (2014, January). The challenges of Challenge.gov: Adopting private sector business innovations in the Federal Government. *2014 47th Hawaii International Conference on System Sciences* (pp. 2073–2082), Waikoloa, HI.

Nevo, D., Kotlarsky, J., & Nevo, S. (2012). New capabilities: Can IT service providers leverage crowdsourcing?. *33rd International Conference on Information Systems*, Orlando, FL.

Nickerson, R. C., Varshney, U., & Muntermann, J. (2013). A method for taxonomy development and its application in information systems. *European Journal of Information Systems*, *22*(3), 336–359.

Oliveira, F., Ramos, I., & Santos, L. (2010, July). Definition of a crowdsourcing innovation service for the European SMEs. *International Conference on Web Engineering* (pp. 412–416), Berlin, Heidelberg.

Poetz, M. K., & Schreier, M. (2012). The value of crowdsourcing: Can users really compete with professionals in generating new product ideas? *Journal of Product Innovation Management, 29*(2), 245–256.

Porta, M., House, B., Buckley, L., & Blitz, A. (2008). Value 2.0: Eight new rules for creating and capturing value from innovative technologies. *Strategy & Leadership, 36*(4), 10–18.

Rajala, R., Westerlund, M., Vuori, M., & Hares, J. P. (2013). From idea crowdsourcing to managing user knowledge. *Technology Innovation Management Review, 3*(12), 23–31.

Redi, J. A., Hoßfeld, T., Korshunov, P., Mazza, F., Povoa, I., & Keimel, C. (2013, October). Crowdsourcing-based multimedia subjective evaluations: a case study on image recognizability and aesthetic appeal. *Proceedings of the 2nd ACM international workshop on Crowdsourcing for multimedia* (pp. 29–34), Barcelona, Spain.

Rich, P. (1992). The organizational taxonomy: Definition and design. *Academy of Management Review, 17*(4), 758–781.

Rogstadius, J., Kostakos, V., Kittur, A., Smus, B., Laredo, J., & Vukovic, M. (2011). An assessment of intrinsic and extrinsic motivation on task performance in crowdsourcing markets. *Proceedings of the International AAAI Conference on Web and Social Media* (Vol. 5, No. 1, pp. 321–328), Atlanta, GA.

Rosen, P. A. (2011). Crowdsourcing lessons for organizations. *Journal of Decision Systems, 20*(3), 309–324.

Rouse, A. C., (2010). A preliminary taxonomy of crowdsourcing. *Proceedings of the Australiasian Conference on Information Systems*, Brisbane, Australia.

Saleh, A., & Julia, S. (2019). Crowdsourcing as one of the innovative tools for higher education development. *International Journal of Educational Research, 2*(10), 11–21.

Schenk, E., & Guittard, C. (2011). Towards a characterization of crowdsourcing practices. *Journal of Innovation Economics Management*, (1), 93–107.

Shao, B., Shi, L., Xu, B., & Liu, L. (2012). Factors affecting participation of solvers in crowdsourcing: An empirical study from China. *Electronic Markets, 22*(2), 73–82.

Sivula, A., & Kantola, J. (2015). Ontology focused crowdsourcing management. *Procedia Manufacturing, 3*, 632–638.

Sloane, P. (2011). *A guide to open innovation and crowdsourcing: Advice from leading experts in the field*. Kogan Page Publishers.

Stewart, O., Huerta, J. M., & Sader, M. (2009, June). Designing crowdsourcing community for the enterprise. *Proceedings of the ACM SIGKDD Workshop on Human Computation* (pp. 50–53), Paris, France.

Surowiecki, J. (2004). *The wisdom of crowds: Why the many are smarter than the few and how collective wisdom shapes business, economies, societies and nations*. Doubleday & Co.

Terwiesch, C., & Xu, Y. (2008). Innovation contests, open innovation, and multiagent problem solving. *Management Science, 54*(9), 1529–1543.

Vakkari, P. (2003). Task-based information searching. *Annual Review of Information Science and Technology, 37*, 413–464.

Vecchia, G. L., & Cisternino, A. (2010). Collaborative workforce, business process crowdsourcing as an alternative of BPO. In F. Daniel, & F. M. Facca (Eds.), *International Conference on Web Engineering* (pp. 425–430). Springer.

Vukovic, M. (2009, July). Crowdsourcing for enterprises. *2009 Congress on Services-I* (pp. 686–692), Los Angeles, CA.

Vukovic, M., & Bartolini, C. (2010). Towards a research agenda for enterprise crowdsourcing. In T. Margaria, & B. Steffen (Eds.), *International symposium on leveraging applications of formal methods, verification and validation* (pp. 425–434). Springer.

Vuurens, J. B., & De Vries, A. P. (2012). Obtaining high-quality relevance judgments using crowdsourcing. *IEEE Internet Computing*, *16*(5), 20–27.

Whitla, P. (2009). Crowdsourcing and its application in marketing activities. *Contemporary Management Research*, *5*(1), 1–14.

Xu, Y., Ribeiro-Soriano, D. E., & Gonzalez-Garcia, J. (2015). Crowdsourcing, innovation and firm performance. *Management Decision*, *53*(6), 1158–1169.

Yang, J., Adamic, L. A., & Ackerman, M. S. (2008, July). Crowdsourcing and knowledge sharing: strategic user behavior on taskcn. *Proceedings of the 9th ACM Conference on Electronic Commerce* (pp. 246–255), Chicago, IL.

Ye, H., & Kankanhalli, A. (2013). Leveraging crowdsourcing for organizational value co-creation. *Communications of the Association for Information Systems*, *33*(1), 13.

Zhang, H., Ma, Y., & Sugiyama, M. (2015). Bandit-based task assignment for heterogeneous crowdsourcing. *Neural Computation*, *27*(11), 2447–2475.

Zhao, Y., & Zhu, Q. (2014). Evaluation on crowdsourcing research: Current status and future direction. *Information Systems Frontiers*, *16*(3), 417–434.

Zogaj, S., Bretschneider, U., & Leimeister, J. M. (2014). Managing crowdsourced software testing: A case study based insight on the challenges of a crowdsourcing intermediary. *Journal of Business Economics*, *84*(3), 375–405.

4 Boosting Innovation of Higher Education Institutions with Crowdsourcing

Regina Lenart-Gansiniec

4.1 Crowdsourcing in Higher Education Institutions as a Driver of Innovations

Crowdsourcing is a concept of increasing importance both in the economic and public environment. While crowdsourcing in business organizations is combined with the possibility of innovative problem solving, business process improvement, and achieving and maintaining a competitive advantage, crowdsourcing in higher education institutions is equally important. Propagators of crowdsourcing in higher education institutions (HEIs) believe that it can be useful for gaining ideas, opinions, feedback from the virtual community, gaining support for various projects, as well as improving communication between individual stakeholders, and even collecting data as part of scientific research, creating textbooks and raising funds for educational projects (Solemon et al., 2013).

One of the reasons crowdsourcing is so promising in terms of innovation stems from the fact that it enables the acquisition of new knowledge from a wide range of participants. Besides, innovations in HEI can be top-down, so imposed by voluntary participation, or bottom-up, that is, they can be initiated because leaders are dissatisfied with a given circumstance (Fullan, 2007). Whether the innovation is imposed or voluntary, the process of change requires access to a variety of knowledge resources. Additionally, another aspect of fostering innovation in education relates to the need to create a collaborative work environment at universities. Finally, the necessity to use technologies is recognized all the time and seen as drivers of university development (Thomas, 2009). At the interface between knowledge, cooperation and technology, crowdsourcing appears as a promising process enabling the creation and implementation of innovations.

Firstly, virtual communities are more diverse in terms of knowledge and experiences than the internal units of an organization, and with the diversity of knowledge comes the opportunity to access more and variety of ideas, ideally resulting in more innovative ideas. Virtual communities have the potential to create and work out new solutions. The knowledge

DOI: 10.4324/9781003227175-5

in their possession may contribute to the creation of new services or improvement of the existing ones (Llorente & Morant, 2015).

Secondly, crowdsourcing makes external entities a source of innovation. Organizations can access not only ideas but also suggestions from all interested parties, contributing to the generation of new ideas. The literature indicates that crowdsourcing platforms facilitate access to tacit knowledge of customers and allow marketing of products that meet their requirements (Anderson, 2011).

Crowdsourcing not only improves access to different knowledge connections, which in turn increases experience, learning by doing and the ability to integrate accumulated knowledge. It is also a tool to support creative people and shape an environment that encourages knowledge management and the appropriation of results. It can, therefore, be concluded that crowdsourcing stimulates creativity, stimulating new thoughts, reformulating existing knowledge and analysing many different assumptions in order to form new ideas. All this makes it possible to create service innovations in HEI thanks to crowdsourcing.

Moreover, the necessity of cooperation of higher education with the environment becomes a necessity, according to which in the changing knowledge-based economy it is necessary not only to strengthen the existing ties between universities and the labour market but also to create new ones. It involves establishing relationships with the environment and including the environment in solving problems or creating innovation. It also allows the university to implement postulates of university openness and transparency. Collaboration and commitment are also the basis and building block of innovation. HEIs opening to the environment, creating and searching for new solutions outside of its own R&D departments makes the resulting innovations more valuable (Jiang et al., 2018).

Cooperation with online communities may be a natural consequence of these guidelines (Llorente & Morant, 2015). In this approach, crowdsourcing gains importance, in particular, due to its potential in terms of the possibility of not only acquiring resources from many sources of human knowledge, which are outside the organization (Brabham, 2008; Howe, 2006, 2008; Lodge & Wegrich, 2014, 2015), but also customer involvement, creating innovation and increasing institutional legitimacy (Liu, 2017, 2021).

In innovations, the issue of reaching for the knowledge and ideas of external partners is important. They are thus involved in creating innovations or sharing ideas with others. In the course of these activities, external knowledge is obtained, mainly from business partners, and joint development of innovations. It is also important to collaborate with specialists outside the organization, and it is important to benefit from open access to ideas and purchase solutions from others. This allows organizations to cooperate within the innovation network, which affects the effectiveness of innovation. Crowdsourcing also meets those needs. Crowdsourcing allows integration of external stakeholders who are a more valuable source of ideas than internal experts (Zhang & Huang, 2022).

Thanks to crowdsourcing, universities can shape and maintain a competitive advantage, gain access to many different ideas for improvement, streamlining and enhancement of universities, build their reputation and become innovative. Crowdsourcing initiatives can contribute to the fact that university management can listen to students and lecturers, which facilitates a multi-perspective view of many issues. Leaders gain a new way to save money and time. Additionally, openness to ideas and changes makes the university much more attractive for future students (Zahirović Suhonjić et al., 2019).

Finally, it must not be forgotten that HEI employees can also become a source of valuable knowledge and ideas for the organization. In this context, internal crowdsourcing becomes more important. The basic idea of internal crowdsourcing is to activate, mobilize and strengthen the internal exchange of knowledge and interaction in the organization. Internal crowdsourcing involves inclusion of employees and associates of the organization in the search for ideas for solving organizational problems (Byrén, 2013) through inter-departmental and interdisciplinary thinking and the ability to jointly work out new solutions, processes and decisions. In this approach, employees of an organization often have comprehensive knowledge, especially tacit knowledge about customers, products and services (Henttonen et al., 2017). Thus, internal crowdsourcing opens the innovation process, enabling the development of ideas and innovations not only by the employees of the research and development department, but also by all employees of the company. For example, employees can develop new business areas or develop incremental innovation.

4.2 Higher Education Practices of Crowdsourcing for Innovations

Universities around the world increasingly seem to recognize the importance of virtual communities and try to engage them in various projects, in particular on an open invitation – via crowdsourcing platforms. It turns out that the knowledge, experience or potential that are in the possession of virtual communities may turn out to be useful and beneficial for the functioning of HEI (Bargfrede et al., 2021; Korir et al., 2022; Kuzminska, 2016).

The above-mentioned types of crowdsourcing practices and their examples are presented below (Doroudi et al., 2018; Kuzminska, 2016). It should be emphasized, however, that it is not the intention of the authors to attempt at recording all crowdsourcing initiatives. When discussing the initiatives in question, the criteria of originality and uniqueness were taken into account, as well as the possibility of their implementation to the conditions of the university in various cultural contexts. A review of crowdsourcing initiatives shows that the potential of crowdsourcing translates into its popularity in universities, especially in the United States. Among the popular areas of application, there is crowdsourcing for new ideas, services and new solutions. Potential possibilities of using internal crowdsourcing for innovations development were also discussed.

4.2.1 Crowdsourcing for New Ideas

Crowdsourcing can be used to search for ideas – in this sense, an organization engages and encourages its clients to participate more actively while generating ideas. There is a greater chance of success for new solutions. It comes down to the fact that a group of people with common interests, goals, but different experiences, knowledge or skills enter into social interactions in order to search for ideas for solving a problem (Pedersen et al., 2013). Crowdsourcing is becoming a kind of knowledge marketplace with rules, interactions, specific duration, methods of assessment and motivation of the virtual community to act (Pedersen et al., 2013; Zogaj et al., 2014). Thanks to this, university can ask the virtual community for ideas and solutions related to strategic planning or development strategy (Dunlap & Lowenthal, 2018).

- Project initiated in October 2010 at California State University, Fullerton campus. The university invited students, faculty and other staff to submit ideas for the development of the campus. Potential interested parties could submit their ideas via e-mail and a website specially created for this purpose.
- In 2010, the UNED University in Spain, through a crowdsourcing platform, obtained ideas from students, scientists, management and administration employees for the development of the university and the creation of a strategic plan.
- In 2011, Columbia University initiated the *What to Fix Columbia* project to gather ideas from students to reduce college bureaucracy.

4.2.2 Crowdsourcing for New Services

Crowdsourcing can be used to test, create products, services or content. The list of possibilities of using this type of crowdsourcing by universities is unlimited: from creating databases, providing assistance, to tagging, ending with creating textbooks – so wherever there is a need for improvement. These activities are usually spontaneous and can contribute to lowering the operating costs associated with the permanent employment of support staff (Alenezi & Faisal, 2020; Rakitina-Qureshi, 2015).

- In 2008, the University of Oxford initiated the crowdsourcing project "The Great War Archive". Internet users from all over the world were invited to participate, and they were asked to fill in the gaps in

the collections and to build a collection of artifacts related to World War I through a special application. In the period from March 2008 to June 2008, over 6,500 different objects were collected. The project was awarded at the Times Higher Educational Awards 2008 in the "Outstanding ICT Initiatives" category.
- In 2016, the University of Oxford announced a crowdsourcing initiative called Transcribe Europeana 1914-1918. It was related to the virtual community's transcription of handwritten texts from World War I and the identification of elements unrecognized during document scanning (electronic reading). Less than a month after the launch of this initiative, over 9,800 documents were submitted, of which over 1,000 are under verification, and over 600 have been decoded by the virtual community.
- In 2009, a crowdsourcing project entitled "Tech Support", where the virtual community became the operator of the "help desk" line (https://kb.iu.edu). The university – instead of investing in this type of solution and employing IT specialists – engaged Internet users to help each other. The inquiries mainly concern IT problems such as: failure of electronic indexes, damaged files or recovery of deleted e-mails. Since the implementation of crowdsourcing, over 15,000 responses have been generated, while the site has over 18 million views per year. A similar solution was implemented by the University of Notre Dame.
- The Meta Data Games project (http://metadatagames.org), initiated in 2011 at the Ludwig and Maximilian University in Munich, aimed to invite the virtual community to tag archival objects with tags. The virtual community could do it by participating in the game and while playing they were entering multimedia collections of a museum or library.
- In 2012, at the Ludwig and Maximilian University in Munich, traditional linguistic field research was replaced by the crowdsourcing project "Metropolitalia" (http://www.metropolitalia.org). Its aim was to involve Italian "native speakers" in the collection of linguistic data from different geographical areas in Italy. As part of the project, the game "Borsa Parole" was prepared. It involved sharing new or existing Italian phrases with other users, and the person adding a given phrase was asked to indicate in which geographic region it was used.
- In 2014, the Language Observatory of the University of Warsaw initiated the project "Latest Polish vocabulary". Its purpose is to register new words that are used on a daily basis but are not found in dictionaries – thus creating an online dictionary of the newest words (over 2,500 words were registered by December 2016).

Crowdsourcing is also used to create textbooks and training materials for students. There is a lot of interest in this area: Online Textbook project (Brigham Young University, book on project management), Crowdsourcing Textbooks (University of North Carolina, book on computer science), Management Through Collaboration Book Project (St John's University, book on management by collaboration), The North Carolina Support Our Students (SOS) Classroom (University of South Carolina, material for primary school students: English as a second language, Arts, Maths and Music).

4.2.3 Crowdsourcing for a New Solution

Ordering Internet users to choose the best solutions, gathering opinions and judgments on a given topic (crowdvoting) is another type of crowdsourcing. In June 2012, the "Innovation Station" project was launched at Davenport University to record, vote and implement virtual community ideas for innovation, organizational change and university improvement. In the same year, the University of Utah organized a "Utah-Based" crowdsourcing competition to submit films on innovative digital media. The prize offered was $25,000. In 2013, the University of Southern Illinois in Carbondale initiated a cyclical crowdsourcing project called "Saluki App", which engaged students in creating applications for mobile devices. The submitted ideas were commented on and evaluated by the virtual community. A winner was also selected. There was a prize of $1,200 along with the opportunity to implement the rewarded idea.

4.3 Possibilities of Crowdfunding Used to Finance Higher Education Institutions

Relevant literature highlights differences between crowdsourcing and crowdfunding. However, due to the possibility of obtaining funds for implementing innovations, crowdfunding becomes of key importance in the context of HEI (Teixeira & Landoni, 2017). Crowdfunding can be a way for universities not only to obtain funds but also to verify the ideas suggested by the virtual community. A huge number of implemented projects, mainly in the United States, may suggest some interest in obtaining additional financial support. Those projects predominantly concern raising funds for science, scholarships, research projects, research and student mobility:

- One of the projects, "Takeashine" (http://takeashine.org), was launched in June 2011. The organizers' goal was to raise funds for education for poor students. Another project called Generation Education (http://educationgeneration.org) aimed at raising money for scholarships for students from Afghanistan, Ecuador, Ghana, Kenya, India, Pakistan, Peru, Rwanda, Sri Lanka and Uganda.
- Apart from fundraising for students, projects related to raising funds for scientific research are initiated. An example can be provided by the "Microryza" platform (https://experiment.com/press), which was launched in April 2012. The platform can be used by scientists who

wish to submit their research projects and receive donations for their launch. At the end of the research, scientists are required to share the results obtained. Since its launch, over 600 projects have been funded; over $7 million has been raised.
- Salem State crowdfunding is a community fundraising platform open to anyone looking to support schools, programmes, faculties, teams, student groups, or specific university projects that are of much importance to interested parties. Crowdfunding also helps faculty and students undertake innovative curricula that might not otherwise be possible.
- The University of Essex Click to crowdfunding platform is open to students, staff and alumni who can submit their big crowdfunding ideas and projects.

Crowdfunding platforms initiated by universities operate on a similar principle, the goals of which are:

- research funding of academics and students ("PitchFunder"; University of Arizona; "CMU"; Carnegie Mellon University; "Cornell"; Cornell University; "Waves of Impact"; Pepperdine University; "OwlCrowd"; Temple University; "Haas School of Crowdfunding"; University of California at Berkeley; "UCLA Spark"; University of California Los Angeles; "UCSF Crowdfunding"; University of California San Francisco; "LAUNCH UMD"; University of Maryland Baltimore; "VOLstarter", University of Tennessee; Knoxville; "Launch UTSA"; University of Texas at San Antonio; "USEED at U.Va."; University of Virginia; "USEED@UW"; University of Washington);
- funding sports teams ("Igite"; Lehigh University; "Ignite Ole Miss"; University of Mississippi);
- funding scholarships for science and sports ("Schreyer Honors College"; Pennsylvania State University; "Ignite USC"; University of Southern California);
- financing student mobility ("MiddSTART"; Middlebury College; "Ignite"; University of Connecticut);
- financing the construction of an innovation studio on the campus ("The Robert A. Foisie '56 Innovation Studio"; Worcester Polytechnic Institute).

Additionally, the following can be listed in the context of crowdfunding platforms:

- GiveCampus – an education fundraising platform that enables HEIs to connect with stakeholders. Graduates, students, parents, lecturers and other employees can establish and maintain contact with the university and support its various activities. Each university has its own guidelines on who and on what terms can create a crowdfunding campaign.

- ScaleFunder – a community engagement fundraising platform focused on attracting new donors. ScaleFunder shows the unique identity of HEIs. The platform was purchased and is managed by the university, and it is the university authorities who decide on the terms on which projects can be presented to a wide group of potential donors.
- USEED – a platform for collecting funds from parties interested in the functioning of a university. Students, lecturers and graduates become university advocates who help in obtaining donations both from the internal community and from people outside the university.

Bearing in mind the examples presented above, crowdfunding can be used by HEI not only to supplement and/or supplement financial resources for educational purposes but also to support the creation of innovation by offering new sources of capital and to enable the crowd to participate in the innovation process by providing feedback to HEI. The feedback is a kind of acceptance – when something gets financed.

To summarize, creating innovation requires external and internal unique knowledge and openness, the latter of which seems to be the fastest way to supplement the missing knowledge resources. In this context, innovation can be considered as a product of learning undertaken in the process of solving a specific problem on the basis of existing knowledge or enriching it with new knowledge. Organizations deciding to implement innovation processes must have easy, cheap and quick access to up-to-date resources of their own and other organizations' knowledge. In this context, crowdsourcing becomes essential. This is due to the fact that the crowdsourcing foundations are provided by the wisdom of the crowd and the use of ideas, resources and competences of people who are interested in solving problems or creating new products/services. It is recognized that a group can achieve and work out more benefits than any expert (Doroudi et al., 2018; Hall & Griffy-Brown, 2016).

References

Alenezi, H. S., & Faisal, M. H. (2020). Utilizing crowdsourcing and machine learning in education: Literature review. *Education and Information Technologies, 25*(4), 2971–2986.

Anderson, M. (2011). Crowdsourcing higher education: A design proposal for distributed learning. *MERLOT Journal of Online Learning and Teaching, 7*(4), 576–590.

Bargfrede, S., Carlson, A., Finning, J., Mammano, M., Ward, A., & Mazzeo, A. (2021, October). Constructing the ideal components of crowdsourcing platforms for higher education. *2021 IEEE MIT Undergraduate Research Technology Conference* (pp. 1–5), Cambridge, MA.

Brabham, D. C. (2008). Crowdsourcing as a model for problem solving: An introduction and cases. *Convergence, 14*(1), 75–90.

Byrén, E. (2013). Internal crowdsourcing for innovation development. How multinational companies can obtain the advantages of crowdsourcing utilising internal resources [Master's thesis]. Chalmers University of Technology.

Doroudi, S., Williams, J., Kim, J., Patikorn, T., Ostrow, K., Selent, D., Heffernan, N. T., Hills, T., & Rosé, C. (2018). Crowdsourcing and education: Towards a theory and praxis of learner sourcing. In J. Kay, & R. Luckin (Eds.), *Rethinking learning in the digital age: Making the learning sciences count, 13th International conference of the learning sciences, international society of the learning sciences*. International Society of the Learning Sciences.

Dunlap, J., & Lowenthal, P. (2018). Online educators' recommendations for teaching online: Crowdsourcing in action. *Open Praxis, 10*(1), 79–89.

Fullan, M. (2007). Change theory as a force for school improvement. In J. M. Burger, C. F. Webber, & P. Klinck (Eds.), *Intelligent leadership* (pp. 27–39). Springer.

Hall, O. P., Jr., & Griffy-Brown, C. (2016). Crowdsourcing management education assessment. *Journal of International Technology and Information Management, 25*(2), 1.

Henttonen, K., Rissanen, T., Eriksson, P., & Hallikas, J. (2017). Cultivating the wisdom of personnel through internal crowdsourcing. *International Journal of Information Technology and Management, 16*(2), 117–132.

Howe, J. (2006). The rise of crowdsourcing. *Wired Magazine, 14*(6), 1–4.

Howe, J. (2008). *Crowdsourcing: How the power of the crowd is driving the future of business*. Random House.

Jiang, Y., Schlagwein, D., & Benatallah, B. (2018). A review on crowdsourcing for education: State of the art of literature and practice. *Pacific Asia Conference on Information Systems*, Yokohama, Japan.

Korir, M., Slade, S., Holmes, W., & Rienties, B. (2022). Eliciting students' preferences for the use of their data for learning analytics: A crowdsourcing approach. In B. Rienties, R. Hampel, E. Scanlon, & D. Whitelock (Eds.), *Open world learning: research, innovation and the challenges of high-quality education* (pp. 144–156). Routledge.

Kuzminska, O. (2016). Crowdsourcing and higher education. *Відкрите освітнє е-середовище сучасного університету, 2*, 39–49.

Liu, H. K. (2017). Crowdsourcing government: Lessons from multiple disciplines. *Public Administration Review, 77*, 656–667. https://doi.org/10.1111/puar.12808

Liu, H. K. (2021). Crowdsourcing: Citizens as coproducers of public services. *Policy & Internet, 13*(2), 315–331.

Llorente, R., & Morant, M. (2015). Crowdsourcing in higher education. In F. J. Garrigos-Simon, I. Gil-Pechuán, & S. Estelles-Miguel (Eds.), *Advances in crowdsourcing* (pp. 87–95). Springer.

Lodge, M., & Wegrich, K. (2014). *The problem solving capacity of the modern state: Governance challenges and administrative capacities*. Oxford University Press.

Lodge, M., & Wegrich, K. (2015). Crowdsourcing and regulatory reviews: A new way of challenging red tape in British government? *Regulation & Governance, 9*(1), 30–46.

Pedersen, J., Kocsis, D., Tripathi, A., Tarrell, A., Weerakoon, A., Tahmasbi, N., & De Vreede, G. J. (2013, January). Conceptual foundations of crowdsourcing: A review of IS research. *2013 46th Hawaii International Conference on System Sciences* (pp. 579–588), Wailea, HI.

Rakitina-Qureshi, E. (2015). Crowdsourcing–a bridge between academia and commerce. *Journal of International Scientific Publications, 13*, 553–561.

Solemon, B., Ariffin, I., Din, M. M., & Anwar, R. M. (2013). A review of the uses of crowdsourcing in higher education. *International Journal of Asian Social Science, 3*(9), 2066–2073.

Teixeira, P., & Landoni, P. (2017). The rise of private higher education. In P. N. Teixeira, S. Kim, & Z. Gilani (Eds.), *Rethinking the public-private mix in higher education* (pp. 21–34). Sense Publishers

Thomas, I. (2009). Critical thinking, transformative learning, sustainable education, and problem-based learning in universities. *Journal of Transformative Education*, 7(3), 245–264.

Zahirović Suhonjić, A., Despotović-Zrakić, M., Labus, A., Bogdanović, Z., & Barać, D. (2019). Fostering students' participation in creating educational content through crowdsourcing. *Interactive Learning Environments*, 27(1), 72–85.

Zhang, M., & Huang, Z. (2022). Crowdsourcing used in higher education: An empirical study on a sustainable translation teaching mode based on crowdsourced translation. *Sustainability*, 14(6), 3140.

Zogaj, S., Bretschneider, U., & Leimeister, J. M. (2014). Managing crowdsourced software testing: A case study based insight on the challenges of a crowdsourcing intermediary. *Journal of Business Economics*, 84(3), 375–405.

5 Innovations in Knowledge Through Crowdsourcing

Łukasz Sułkowski

5.1 Knowledge Management

When looking for sources of development, crowdsourcing in HEIs cannot ignore the knowledge and information management trend that has been developing since the 1970s and is gaining momentum along with the crystallization of the digital university formation. Mission of each university involves production, reproduction, transmission, dissemination and application of knowledge, which places the issues of knowledge and information management at the centre of interest of higher education institutions (Kalkan, 2017). The challenge of modern universities is precisely to develop the concept of knowledge and information management that allows for effective first stream filling (Alexandropoulou et al., 2009). Knowledge management methods are developing faster and faster in conjunction with information and communication technologies (ICT). Digitization, computerization, decision-making based on data and countability are just selected examples of the directions of development of modern universities closely related to knowledge management (Omona et al., 2010). The use of next generations of information technologies allows not only for accumulating, processing and transferring knowledge more and more effectively but also for increasing the efficiency of work and organization. The reasons for the growing importance of knowledge management processes include profound transformation of societies and economies, acceleration of the pace of data, information and knowledge production, data and information overload, problems with data selection and evaluation, increased competition, deepening specialization, and hindrance of the critical assessment of knowledge (Serban & Luan, 2002).

Knowledge management focuses on the processes, methods and practices of creating, acquiring, sharing and using knowledge, wherever it is, in order to strengthen the effectiveness of the organization's activities and learning processes (Sarmadi et al., 2017a, 2017b; Sedziuviene & Vveinhardt, 2009). Knowledge is meaningful and reliable information, while information is organized data (Davenport & Prusak, 1998). Knowledge in organizations, including universities, takes various forms, ranging from explicit to tacit

DOI: 10.4324/9781003227175-6

knowledge (Johannessen et al., 2001). There are several goals for knowledge management:

- creating new knowledge,
- gaining access to knowledge from external sources,
- using knowledge in decision-making processes,
- knowledge reproduction,
- disseminating knowledge,
- reflecting knowledge in documents, databases and software,
- stimulating the development of knowledge
- transfer of knowledge within the organization,
- embedding knowledge in processes, products, systems, concepts and methods,
- measuring and assessing the value of information resources and the impact on management (Alexandropoulou et al., 2009; Evans et al., 2015; Halawi et al., 2006).

The role of management in these processes is not limited to control processes only. It includes activities related to organizing, promoting the creation and sharing knowledge, which should lead to the development of learning, intelligent and knowledge-oriented organizations (Alvarenga Neto et al., 2009; Shaabani et al., 2012).

5.2 Knowledge Management in HEIs

Knowledge management concepts can be associated with many concepts of management science (Grant, 2000). At the strategic level, one can refer to the resource school, indicating that knowledge resources and their proper use are the most important source of competitive advantage. Having and using valuable, unique and non-imitating knowledge resources is the strategic goal of an organization in a competitive market (Choi & Lee, 2002). In higher education, knowledge management is clearly understood as the core of all organizational processes (Al-Zoubi, 2014; Slater & Moreton, 2007). In particular, this applies to the new forms of university: entrepreneurial, digital, intelligent, virtual (Bratianu, 2020; Secundo et al., 2019; Vallé et al., 2016).

Universities also implement selected concepts of strategic management using methods derived from business, such as balanced scorecard (BSC), sector analysis, creating strategic maps (Chen et al., 2006; Hladchenko, 2015; Pietrzak et al., 2015). From the marketing point of view, knowledge management can lead to innovation, co-creating market value with the customer, shaping communication with the market, exerting influence on customers (Shaw et al., 2001). The rapid development of partner and relationship marketing is also possible thanks to the implementation of information and communication concepts and tools (Rowley, 2004). Reliable information and knowledge are key to building a market position (Tsai & Shih, 2004). Knowledge management is done by connecting people with technology and organization. In the functional area of human resource management, a profound change has also been taking place for several decades (Yahya & Goh, 2002). The general tendency to be quantifiable and to base decisions on data also applies to people and intellectual resources in universities (Svetlik & Stavrou-Costea, 2007). They should lead to an increase in the competences and motivation to work of university employees, which is modelled on business solutions and public organizations shaped in accordance with the new public management approach. Thanks to the expansion of HR systems, competences, work results, achievements and contribution to the organization's activities are measured and compared (Brewer & Brewer, 2010). Universities are also introducing human capital management methods developed in enterprises, such as talent management, data-based human resource management, highly efficient HR systems, reengineering, job sharing (Madsen & Slåtten, 2017). In practice, the introduction of business models in managing people in academic cultures raises considerable resistance can be a source of frustration and, frequently, does not lead to any increase in work efficiency (Adler et al., 2007). The area of quality management in universities as well as process and project management (PM) are also linked to the development of knowledge and information management (Zinzou & Doctor, 2020). Evidence-based and data-based decision-making and effective control over organizational processes and projects are developing thanks to the implementation of knowledge management concepts, which takes the form of specialized information and communication systems at universities (Bührig et al., 2018). These are just a few selected areas of management in which knowledge management is applicable. Knowledge management in universities is also related to the issues of: innovation (Ngoc-Tan & Gregar, 2018), leadership (Rehman & Iqbal, 2020), organizational culture (Omerzel et al., 2011), risk management (Ruzic-Dimitrijevic & Dakic, 2014), didactics (Altinay et al., 2019; Popescu, 2017), research (Loh et al., 2003; Zhao, 2003). Knowledge management applications are developing both in the private and public sectors (Ramachandran et al., 2013; Razzaq et al., 2019).

5.3 Types of Knowledge in HEIs

A cognitively useful look may also take into account knowledge taxonomies that can be applied to universities. This is just one of the many taxonomies, typologies and classifications found in the literature on the subject (Geisler, 2007). Its use to understand knowledge management in universities is supported by its simplicity and universality, allowing it to be used in very different types of activity. The classic differentiation between tacit and explicit knowledge, first developed by Polanyi (1967), is also reflected in the academic world. Tacit knowledge is contextual, rooted in action, experience and commitment. Tacit knowledge can be divided into a mental model and a technical model (Alavi & Leidner, 2001). An example of knowledge hidden in the mental model can be various aspects of individual and collective identity in the academic world, such as knowledge of the academic ethos and understanding the traditional culture of the university (Zamani, 2021). Tacit technical knowledge is an answer to the question of how to do something under certain conditions, it is a kind of specialist knowledge of things that is habitual and intuitive (know-how). The unfamiliar communication skills of the academic community (Tian et al., 2009) can be an exemplification. Explicit knowledge is conscious, articulated and communicated, it is often collected, stored and transferred by IT systems. In the academic world, scientific and didactic publications, internal university regulations, all documentation and all formalized content are part of open knowledge (Butnariu & Milosan, 2012). The second type of typology is the individual versus social dichotomy. The former, created by individuals and maintained individually, is not passed on in communication processes, although, of course, it can be used in relationships with other people. Individual, non-disseminated opinions and knowledge of others, which can also be used in the academic world to play games for power and resources, is a good example here. Social knowledge is co-created, modified and communicated by the social group. This type is dominant in universities, which are obviously organizations and purposeful social groups. The level of socialization of knowledge may vary, ranging from that co-created in a group and communicated, to that created individually and only transferred. Works created jointly by students, scientific publications and diploma theses – written in co-authorship or in cooperation with the supervisor, teaching materials that are disseminated and modified under the influence of group opinion are just a few of the possible types of social knowledge. Declared knowledge is of a social nature and is a kind of demonstration that someone has control over an information resource (know-about). It may be the declared and demonstrated knowledge of power relations in universities, which allows for obtaining organizational influence (Khan et al., 2012). Procedural knowledge is the knowledge of the process of acquiring knowledge (know-how) (Wipawayangkool & Teng, 2016). An example is provided by formalized communication in the form of university organizational procedures as part of the internal education quality management system (Fenton-O'Creevy et al., 2006). Causal knowledge is causal in nature and is an answer to the questions of why and how (know-how). Its heuristic nature results from the ability to understand reality. Cause-and-effect understanding is a key cognitive skill in a human being. Research shows that the homo sapiens species is characterized by an evolutionary tendency to seek causal explanations, often not accepting stochastic explanations intuitively (Mitchell, 2008; Rehder and Hastie, 2001). Searching for the reasons for management decisions in universities is usually a mental construct, based on information and interpretations, allowing to discover cause-effect chains with different probability (Olsen & Maassen, 2007). The lower the probability is based on guesswork, the higher the probability is based on hypotheses, and the higher the probability is a certainty. Conditional knowledge, closely related to causal knowledge, focuses on perceiving the conditions when something is happening (know-when) (Zhang et al., 2016). An example may be provided by knowledge about employee evaluation, motivation and development systems, in which the condition for obtaining benefits is the achievement of a measurable result. Relational knowledge can be social or relational in nature and determines relationships, interactions between people or things (know-with). In social relations of the authorities, relations may allow them to gain influence, e.g., in collegiate bodies at universities. Pragmatic knowledge is one that can be used in an organization (Table 5.1). Examples in higher education can refer to good practices, scientific works, teaching materials, internal law.

Table 5.1 Taxonomies of knowledge in universities

Knowledge type	Definition	Examples at universities
Tacit – mental	Contextual knowledge, rooted in action, experience and commitment Mental models	Knowledge of the academic ethos and understanding of the traditional culture of the university
Tacit – technical	Knowledge of how to do something under certain conditions (know-how), tacit specialist knowledge	Unlearned communication skills of the academic community
Public	Articulated, made aware and generalized knowledge	Scientific publications, internal law of universities
Individual	Created by individuals and maintained individually	Individual, non-disseminated opinions
Social	Created and communicated by a social group	Collective publications, group work of students
Declared	Demonstrated, know-about	Declared knowledge about authority relations in the university
Procedural	Knowledge of the process of obtaining knowledge, know how	Organizational procedures at the university
Causal	Understanding why, know why (know-how)	Knowledge of the reasons for staffing decisions at universities
Conditional	Knowing when something is going on, know when	Knowledge of the incentive system and reward mechanisms
Relational	Knowledge of interactions, relationships, know-with	Knowledge about coalitions in decision-making bodies (e.g., the Senate)
Pragmatic	Useful knowledge in the organization	Good practices, scientific works, teaching materials, internal law, etc.

Source: Own study based on Alavi and Leidner (2001).

5.4 Knowledge Management Paradigms in HEIs

When organizing the concepts of knowledge management systems, it is worth looking at them from several perspectives and considering the possibilities of their application in relation to the university. Consistent use of the conceptualization of Alavi and Leidner (2001) will make it possible to abandon the analysis of other paradigms and cognitive perspectives on knowledge management in universities, present in the literature on the subject.

The cybernetic perspective emphasizes the processing of knowledge, information and data that can be provided to people through feedback. In universities, organizational procedures, specialized units (e.g., IT) and positions (e.g., Chief Information Officer [CIO]) serve this purpose. The conditions for the effective functioning of knowledge management systems in universities are not only the systems themselves, competent people and organizational structures but also the identification of the strategic importance of knowledge management and the development of learning-oriented organizational cultures (Sedziuviene & Vveinhardt, 2009). Crowdsourcing in this sense focuses on the acquisition and processing of data in the network by the crowd. The cognitive approach identifies knowledge with a state of mind and focuses on supporting learning and understanding by providing information. The university's IT ecosystem provides access to sources of knowledge: information and data, but it is people's reflection and interpretation that allow them for gaining knowledge. The university seen from the cognitive perspective should be a learning organization; in other words, it ought to be intelligent (Koris et al., 2017). Crowdsourcing of such an organization focuses on learning and gaining new knowledge online by the crowd. The reistic position, inspired by T. Kotarbiński's philosophy, assumes that knowledge is tangible, it is an object that can be accumulated and manipulated (de Monthoux, 2017). Knowledge management will be based on creating and operating on its collections. In universities, such activities are carried out by the IT ecosystem that processes data and information. They include very diverse collections concerning, for example: students, employees, academic achievements, library collections, finances and management decisions (Oprea et al., 2017).

Crowdsourcing understood in reistic terms can refer to management of the knowledge corpus in the network by the crowd (Barbosa & Santos, 2017). The process perspective focuses on the flow and co-creation of knowledge in communication processes, which is universal for any type of organization (Ruoslahti, 2020). Here, crowdsourcing can be understood as a continuous process of co-creating knowledge on the web by the crowd. Co-creation in the social process is an evolving management approach that also applies to university stakeholders. Access is a key social category that enables the use of knowledge (accession approach).

Knowledge management systems involve software used to search for content, data and information that is organized according to an access hierarchy. Universities, like other organizations, use such systems not only for the purpose of collecting and retrieving information but also for creating a multi-level system enabling the exercise of power and management control. Access to information is an emanation of the hierarchy of power. Crowdsourcing can also focus on opening up communication and giving access and participation in network activities within the crowd. Knowledge is also a potential that is realized in action by creating key competences of people and strategic know-how. The university's IT and communication systems strengthen the development of internal stakeholders' competences by providing data and information (Table 5.2). Thus, crowdsourcing is also a development potential for people and organizations in the network by the crowd.

5.5 Information and Communication Technologies in Knowledge in HEIs

Many universities do not have an organized knowledge management system. They even do not understand such a system. Since higher education is about creating and transforming knowledge, such a deficit is striking. However, some colleges and universities are making progress in the implementation of knowledge management concepts and methods and in the development of information and communication systems that allow them to effectively organize those processes (Serban & Luan, 2002).

When conducting knowledge management analysis in universities, it is necessary to move from the level of general taxonomies and perspectives of knowledge understanding to the operational level at which management systems in universities based on ICT operate. These technologies and related information and organizational systems create an increasingly complex and rapidly developing ecosystem with varying degrees of integration. Its functioning includes the following missions: teaching, research and implementation, and increasingly relates to the management of the entire university, both at the strategic and operational levels.

The university's specialized ICT for education include dean's office (student information system), enrolment systems, supporting learning and remote education with e-learning (LMS). The possibility of IT systems realizing such processes as creation, codification, knowledge transfer has developed with the advent of business intelligence (BI) IT systems. Their functionality is based on the theory of knowledge management, but their usability has developed as a result of the technological revolution in the form of cloud computing using mass data sets (big data) from transactional systems, Internet traffic and social networks.

University management systems that are partially used by universities consist of a number of services and products related to organizational concepts. Their implementation and use are possible thanks to the considerable involvement of employees. The division of the software into groups

Table 5.2 Perspectives of knowledge understanding and their application in universities

Perspective	Characteristic	Knowledge management	Knowledge management in universities	Crowdsourcing in HEIs
Cybernetic Knowledge versus information and data	The raw data is unprocessed. Information is processed and interpreted data.	People's access to potentially useful knowledge and making it easier to assimilate.	Strategies, procedures, CIO, IT department, culture of knowledge.	Crowd data acquisition and processing on the web.
Cognitive State of mind	Knowledge is a state of mind and understanding.	Supporting learning and understanding by providing information.	A learning, knowledge-oriented, intelligent organization.	Learning and gaining new knowledge online by crowd.
Reistic Object	Knowledge is an object that can be collected and manipulated.	Building and managing knowledge sets.	The university's IT ecosystem processes data.	Crowd management of the knowledge corpus on the web.
Process Process	Knowledge is the application of cognitive and communication processes to enhance its transfer.	Flow, transfer, co-creation of knowledge.	Knowledge management processes.	The continuous process of co-creating knowledge on the web by the crowd.
Accessible Access to information	Knowledge is necessary to access information.	Organization of access to and acquisition of content.	Access levels and search engines of universities.	Opening and giving access and participation in network activities within the crowd.
Potential Possibilities	Knowledge is a potential that is realized in action.	Key human competences and strategic know-how.	Development and learning of internal stakeholders.	Development potential for people and organizations on the web by the crowd.

Source: Own study based on Alavi and Leidner (2001).

Table 5.3 Methods and concepts used in knowledge management

Name	Abbreviation	Description
Business process management	BPM	The concept that belongs to the organization of process management or business process management.
Business process modelling	BPM	Modelling of business processes. The abbreviation is identical to the previously mentioned concept, but this concept is only some part of it.
Business process reengineering	BPR	Reengineering of business processes, a revolutionary approach to changes in business processes.
Total quality management	TQM	Total quality management, a method of improving the quality of organizational processes.
Continuous process improvement	CPI	Continuous improvement of business processes.
Balanced scorecard	BSC	Balanced scorecard or strategy map methodology. It is about the selective inclusion of goals set by the company in the employee development strategy and the control of their implementation using the Key Performance Indicators (KPIs)

Source: Own study based on Eroshkin et al. (2017).

allows for the emergence of concepts and methods useful in information management in the first place (Table 5.3).

The above-mentioned methods have their implementation tools, among which we can find the following:

- knowledge management (KM) – a knowledge management system that enables the effective implementation of business strategies;
- business process management system (BPMS) – business process management, enabling the implementation of the BPM concept;
- TQM and the use of various languages and notations in modelling business processes;
- BI – a system based on personal computers. Online Analytical Processing is used here, i.e., multidimensional analytical data processing, as well as data mining, i.e., the data mining function, which is also referred to by the term knowledge discovery in databases, meaning intelligent discovery of knowledge in databases;
- project portfolio management (PPM) – a portfolio and PM system, but only PM (e.g., PM systems) can be used;
- corporate performance management (CPM) – CPM system. The term was started by International Data Corporation (IDC) analysts. Hyperion uses a similar concept of enterprise performance management (EPM) – an EPM system. You can also encounter the term of business performance management (BPM) – a BPM system. This abbreviation is used for the third time, and it does not make the concepts easier to understand, but it must be remembered that here it means a separate concept.

The third group of IT systems is used in operational management. It is listed as follows:

- PM;
- computer-aided design (CAD) – CAD of analogue systems, computer technology in design;
- enterprise content management – management of the company's information resources, the state equivalent of EDMS, i.e., an electronic document management system;
- online transaction processing – real-time transaction processing system and other technological control systems, i.e.:
- enterprise resource planning (ERP);
- customer relationships management (CRM);
- supplier relationships management.

The aforementioned systems are adapted by some universities from business to higher education and are used for more effective management of knowledge and information. Among the most frequently used systems in higher education, the following systems can be listed: ERP, BI, PPM, KM and CRM.

5.6 Crowdsourcing and Knowledge

Crowdsourcing is by definition associated with the joint creation of value and knowledge in a group, which gives the possibility of using the achievements of the knowledge management trend. Returning to the description of the essence of crowdsourcing, it is possible to point to its close connection with knowledge management in the times of advanced digital transformation. In their definition of crowdsourcing, E. Estellés-Arolas and F. González-Ladrón-de-Guevara, based on an analysis of 209 publications from the 21st century describe two key characteristics that can be defined as a common field of knowledge management and crowdsourcing.

1 Both approaches emphasize the value of open access and voluntary value creation: "a type of participative online activity in which an individual, an institution, a non-profit organization, or company proposes to a group of individuals of varying knowledge, heterogeneity and number, via a flexible open call, the voluntary undertaking of a task".
2 Both knowledge management and crowdsourcing should bring mutual benefits: the undertaking of the task, of variable complexity and modularity, and in which the crowd should participate bringing their work, money, knowledge and/or experience, always entails mutual benefit (Estellés-Arolas & González-Ladrón-de-Guevara, 2012, pp. 9–10).

Crowdsourcing, seen as a collective way of creating new ventures and knowledge, is therefore closely related to knowledge management as well as innovation. The transmission of this activity into the academic sphere is associated with the reconstruction of knowledge management systems in the direction of digitization, openness, and multifunctionality, which is closely related to the processes of digital transformation of universities.

Digitization refers to the implementation of crowdsourcing in the form of internet communication, interactive and network methods and tools for collecting and analysing data. In HEIs, as in other organizations, this leads to an evidence-based management approach and the development of data-based controlling processes. It also means an increase in digital competency requirements for academic managers, university staff and other stakeholders.

Openness means a shift in knowledge management to an open access approach in most spheres of activity, which is also associated with the multifunctionality of crowdsourcing. Crowdsourcing in science can bring significant benefits in terms of research and publication development. Teaching crowdsourcing can contribute to rapid creation and dissemination of materials to the university, e.g., Mooc's. In the third mission, it can, in turn, become a source of implementation and financial projects as well as new knowledge resources created in cooperation with the non-academic environment. Crowdsourcing is becoming increasingly seen as a source of innovation for higher education. Among researchers and practitioners of crowdsourcing in higher education institutions, the role of data acquisition, analysis, knowledge management and decision-making based on data is emphasized. Sources of knowledge can include feedback from the virtual community, involvement of researchers and stakeholders in collecting data, creating textbooks, and raising funds for educational projects. In the case of the latter, it is indicated that the knowledge resources obtained through crowdsourcing allow for an improvement in the budgeting of institutions and a more effective allocation of time.

Both crowdsourcing and knowledge management have components of spontaneous and controlled processes. In crowdsourcing, the process of designing and accounting for the implementation of tasks is usually planned and controlled, while the selection of participants and their activities can be largely spontaneous. In the case of knowledge management, in which, by definition, we strive to some degree of control over the process, apart from explicit knowledge, we also deal with tacit knowledge that develops spontaneously. It is therefore worth noting that just as knowledge management processes are needed, crowdsourcing should not remain a completely spontaneous process.

In summary, crowdsourcing reflects the processes of deepening digital transformation and focuses on creating and disseminating knowledge in an open network. In the higher education sector, whose mission is to create and transmit knowledge, crowdsourcing is a source of innovative concepts and methods to improve the effectiveness of knowledge management processes. Thus, academic crowdsourcing acts as an accelerator of innovation in knowledge management in all streams of HEI's activities: education, science and third stream.

References

Adler, P. S., Forbes, L. C., & Willmott, H. (2007). 3 critical management studies. *Academy of Management Annals, 1*(1), 119–179.

Alavi, M., & Leidner, D. E. (2001). Knowledge management and knowledge management systems: Conceptual foundations and research issues. *MIS Quarterly, 25*(1), 107–136.

Alexandropoulou, D. A., Angelis, V. A., & Mavri, M. (2009). Knowledge management and higher education: Present state and future trends. *International Journal of Knowledge and Learning, 5*(1), 96–106.

Altınay, F., Altınay, M., Dagli, G., & Altınay, Z. (2019). A study of knowledge management systems processes and technology in open and distance education institutions in higher education. *International Journal of Information and Learning Technology, 36*(4), 314–321.

Alvarenga Neto, R. C. D., Souza, R. R., Queiroz, J. G., & Chipp, H. (2009). Implementation of a knowledge management process within the Brazilian organizational context: The ONS (National Operator of the Interconnected Power System) experience. *6th International Conference on Intellectual Capital, Knowledge Management and Organisational Learning* (pp. 1–2), Montreal, QC, Canada.

Al-Zoubi, D. M. (2014). Improving teaching and learning at universities-the use of knowledge management. *International Journal of Advanced Corporate Learning, 7*(1), 32.

Barbosa, L. S., & Santos, L. P. (2017, September). Networks of universities as a tool for GCIO education. In M. Janssen, K. Axelsson, O. Glassey, B. Klievink, R. Krimmer, I. Lindgren, P. Parycek, H. J. Scholl, & D. Trutnev (Eds.), *International conference on electronic government* (pp. 117–127). Springer.

Bratianu, C. (2020). Designing knowledge strategies for universities in crazy times. *Management Dynamics in the Knowledge Economy, 8*(3), 209–223.

Brewer, P. D., & Brewer, K. L. (2010). Knowledge management, human resource management, and higher education: A theoretical model. *Journal of Education for Business, 85*(6), 330–335.

Bührig, J., Schoormann, T., & Knackstedt, R. (2018). Business process management in German Institutions of higher education: The case of jade university of applied science. In J. vom Brocke, & J. Mendling (Eds.), *Business process management cases* (pp. 577–592). Springer.

Butnariu, M., & Milosan, I. (2012). Preliminary assessment of knowledge management in universities. *Procedia – Social and Behavioral Sciences, 62*, 791–795.

Chen, S. H., Yang, C. C., & Shiau, J. Y. (2006). The application of balanced scorecard in the performance evaluation of higher education. *The TQM Magazine, 18*, 190–205.

Choi, B., & Lee, H. (2002). Knowledge management strategy and its link to knowledge creation process. *Expert Systems with Applications, 23*(3), 173–187.

Davenport, T., & Prusak, L. (1998). *Working knowledge: How organizations manage what they know*. Harvard Business School Press.

de Monthoux, P. G. (2017). Art, philosophy and business: Turns to speculative realism in European management scholarship. In S. Siebert (Ed.), *Management research: European perspectives* (pp. 87–102). Routledge.

Eroshkin, S. Y., Kameneva, N. A., Kovkov, D., & Sukhorukov, A. (2017). Conceptual system in the modern information management. *Procedia Computer Science, 103*, 609–612.

Estellés-Arolas, E., & Gonzalez-Ladron-de-Guevara, F. (2012). Towards an integrated crowdsourcing definition. *Journal of Information Science, 38* (2), 189–200.

Evans, M., Dalkir, K., & Bidian, C. (2015). A holistic view of the knowledge life cycle: The knowledge management cycle (KMC) model. *The Electronic Journal of Knowledge Management, 12*(1), 47.

Fenton-O'Creevy, M., Knight, P., & Margolis, J. (2006). A practice-centered approach to management education. *New visions of graduate management education* (pp. 103–123). Information Age Publishing.

Geisler, E. (2007). A typology of knowledge management: Strategic groups and role behavior in organizations. *Journal of Knowledge Management, 11*(1), 84–96.

Grant, R. M. (2000). Shifts in The world economy: The drivers of knowledge management. In D. Chauvel, & C. Despres (Eds.), *Knowledge horizons: The present and the promise of knowledge management* (pp. 27–53). Butterworth-Heinemann.

Halawi, L. A., McCarthy, R. V., & Aronson, J. E. (2006). Knowledge management and the competitive strategy of the firm. *The Learning Organization, 13*(4), 384–397.

Hladchenko, M. (2015). Balanced Scorecard – A strategic management system of the higher education institution. *International Journal of Educational Management, 29*(2), 167–176.

Johannessen, J. A., Olaisen, J., & Olsen, B. (2001). Mismanagement of tacit knowledge: The importance of tacit knowledge, the danger of information technology, and what to do about it. *International Journal of Information Management, 21*(1), 3–20.

Kalkan, V. D. (2017). A constructive response to the challenges faced by higher education institutions: University knowledge management. *Asia Pacific Journal of Advanced Business and Social Studies, 3*(1), 180–191.

Khan, M. M., Rehman, Z. U., & Dost, M. K. B. (2012). Effects of dynamics persuading and nurturing the professional learning behaviour of the university students: A knowledge management approach. *Arabian Journal of Business and Management Review, 1*, 1–110.

Koris, R., Örtenblad, A., & Ojala, T. (2017). From maintaining the status quo to promoting free thinking and inquiry: Business students' perspective on the purpose of business school teaching. *Management Learning, 48*(2), 174–186.

Loh, B., Tang, A. C., Menkhoff, T., Chay, Y. W., & Evers, H. D. (2003). Applying knowledge management in university research. *Governing and Managing Knowledge in Asia*, 199–226.

Zhao, F. (2003). Transforming quality in research supervision: A knowledge-management approach. *Quality in Higher Education, 9*(2), 187–197.

Madsen, D., & Slåtten, K. (2017). The rise of HR analytics: A preliminary exploration. *Global Conference on Business and Finance Proceedings, 2*(1), 148–159.

Mitchell, S. D. (2008). Exporting causal knowledge in evolutionary and developmental biology. *Philosophy of Science, 75*(5), 697–706l.

Rehder, B., & Hastie, R. (2001). Causal knowledge and categories: The effects of causal beliefs on categorization, induction, and similarity. *Journal of Experimental Psychology, 130*(3), 323–360.

Ngoc-Tan, N., & Gregar, A. (2018). Impacts of knowledge management on innovations in higher education institutions: An empirical evidence from Vietnam. *Economics and Sociology*, *11*(3), 301–320.

Olsen, J. P., & Maassen, P. (2007). European Debates on the knowledge institution: The modernization of the university at the European level. In *University dynamics and European integration* (pp. 3–22). Springer.

Omerzel, D. G., Biloslavo, R., Trnavčevič, A., & Trnavčevič, A. (2011). Knowledge management and organisational culture in higher education institutions. *Journal for East European Management Studies*, *16*(2), 111–139.

Omona, W., van der Weide, T., & Lubega, J. (2010). Using ICT to enhance knowledge management in higher education: A conceptual framework and research agenda. *International Journal of Education and Development Using ICT*, *6*(4), 83–101.

Oprea, C., Popescu, D. M., Petrescu, A. G., & Barbu, I. (2017). A data mining based model to improve university management. *Journal of Science and Arts*, *17*(2), 285.

Pietrzak, M., Paliszkiewicz, J., & Klepacki, B. (2015). The application of the balanced scorecard (BSC) in the higher education setting of a Polish university. *Online Journal of Applied Knowledge Management*, *3*(1), 151–164.

Polanyi, M. (1967). Sense-giving and sense-reading. *Philosophy*, *42*(162), 301–325.

Popescu, G. H. (2017). Organizational e-learning and knowledge management in higher education. *Journal of Self-Governance and Management Economics*, *5*(1), 87–93.

Ramachandran, S. D., Chong, S. C., & Wong, K. Y. (2013). Knowledge management practices and enablers in public universities: A gap analysis. *Campus-Wide Information Systems*, *30*(2).

Razzaq, S., Shujahat, M., Hussain, S., Nawaz, F., Wang, M., Ali, M., & Tehseen, S. (2019). Knowledge management, organizational commitment and knowledge-worker performance: The neglected role of knowledge management in the public sector. *Business Process Management Journal*, *25*(5), 923–947.

Rehman, U. U., & Iqbal, A. (2020). Nexus of knowledge-oriented leadership, knowledge management, innovation and organizational performance in higher education. *Business Process Management Journal*. *26*(6), 1731–1758.

Rowley, J. (2004). Partnering paradigms? Knowledge management and relationship marketing. *Industrial Management & Data Systems*, *104*(2), 149–157.

Ruoslahti, H. (2020). Complexity in project co-creation of knowledge for innovation. *Journal of Innovation & Knowledge*, *5*(4), 228–235.

Ruzic-Dimitrijevic, L., & Dakic, J. (2014). The risk management in higher education institutions. *Online Journal of Applied Knowledge Management*, *2*(1), 137–152.

Sarmadi, M. R., Nouri, Z., Zandi, B., & Lavasani, M. G. (2017a). Academic culture and its role in knowledge management in higher education system. *International Journal of Environmental and Science Education*, *12*(5), 1427–1434.

Sarmadi, M. R., Zandi, B., Nouri, Z., & Lavasani, M. G. (2017b). Information and communication technology and knowledge management in higher education system. *Interdisciplinary Journal of Virtual Learning in Medical Sciences*, *8*(2), 1–8.

Sedziuviene, N., & Vveinhardt, J. (2009). The paradigm of knowledge management in higher educational institutions. *Engineering Economics*, *65*(5), 79–90.

Serban, A. M., & Luan, J. (2002). Overview of knowledge management. *New Directions for Institutional Research*, *113*, 5–16.

Shaabani, E., Ahmadi, H., & Yazdani, H. (2012). Do interactions among elements of knowledge management lead to acquiring core competencies? *Business Strategy Series*, *13*(6), 307–322.

Shaw, M. J., Subramaniam, C., Tan, G. W., & Welge, M. E. (2001). Knowledge management and data mining for marketing. *Decision Support Systems, 31*(1), 127–137.

Slater, A., & Moreton, R. (2007). Knowledge management in higher education: A case study in a large modern UK university. In *Advances in information systems development* (pp. 371–382). Springer.

Secundo, G., Schiuma, G., & Jones, P. (2019). Strategic knowledge management models and tools for entrepreneurial universities. *Management Decision. 57*(12), 3217–3225.

Svetlik, I., & Stavrou-Costea, E. (2007). Connecting human resources management and knowledge management. *International Journal of Manpower, 28*(3/4), 197–206.

Tian, J., Nakamori, Y., & Wierzbicki, A. P. (2009). Knowledge management and knowledge creation in academia: A study based on surveys in a Japanese research university. *Journal of Knowledge Management, 13*, 76–92.

Tsai, M. T., & Shih, C. M. (2004). The impact of marketing knowledge among managers on marketing capabilities and business performance. *International Journal of Management, 21*(4), 524.

Vallé, H. A. C., Peralta, G., Farioli, M., & Giacosa, L. (2016). New paradigms for university management. In *Entrepreneurial and innovative practices in public institutions* (pp. 19–39). Springer.

Wipawayangkool, K., & Teng, J. T. (2016). Assessing tacit knowledge and sharing intention: A knowledge internalization perspective. *Knowledge and Process Management, 23*(3), 194–206.

Yahya, S., & Goh, W. K. (2002). Managing human resources toward achieving knowledge management. *Journal of Knowledge Management, 6*(5), 457–468.

Zamani, A. (2021). Establishing and improving of tacit knowledge sharing network in higher education. *Journal of Studies in Library and Information Science, 13*(4), doi: 10.22055/slis.2021.34442.1773.

Zhang, Y., Song, L., & Huang, W. (2016, April). Research on the college students' competition credit-assisted management system for practical universities. *6th International Conference on Electronic, Mechanical, Information and Management Society* (pp. 167–173). Atlantis Press.

Zinzou, E. F., & Doctor, T. R. (2020). Knowledge management practices among the internal quality assurance network (IQAN)-member higher education Institutions (HEIs) in Thailand. *World Journal of Education, 10*(5), 108–121.

6 How Crowdsourcing Is Changing Innovation
Perspective Post-COVID HEI's

Łukasz Sułkowski

6.1 Impact of Pandemic on Innovations in HEI

The COVID-19 pandemic, according to the common opinion of researchers, has accelerated the processes of digitization and computerization in many sectors. Research shows that global changes to accelerate the pace of digital transformation are occurring in most activities, ranging from healthcare, education and social care, through the information and technology sectors, to manufacturing, trading and other services. Deep changes affect both the private and public sectors, and they relate to small, medium and large organizations. The direction of changes towards virtualization, teleworking, remote management, interactive network communication has been set for many decades, but both the pace and scale of these activities changed in the years 2020–2021, which became one of the consequences of the COVID-19 pandemic. A trend that leaves a lasting change is the deepening digitization of work and education on a global scale, leading to a shift towards hybrid forms of work, even after the COVID-19 pandemic has ended (Meiler, 2020). Research shows that the degree of acceptance, satisfaction and a sense of security from remote work – compared to traditional forms of work – has significantly increased. Most studies indicate that employees, students and students have learned to use remote communication forms and they assume that they will use this competence also after the end of the coronavirus epidemic (Ahmed & Opoku, 2022; McCormack et al., 2021; 239; Savić, 2020; St-Onge et al., 2022):

- knowledge and skills in the field of digitization and computerization of organizations (digital literacy);
- technical knowledge and skills allowing the use of teleworking;
- orientation to permanent learning and personal development (lifelong microlearning and personal development);
- involvement in organizational activities and changes (engagement);
- mobility and readiness to work remotely (mobile force and remote work);
- entering the competences of the digital generation (generation gap);
- accepting and understanding the principles of digital ethics (Savić, 2020).

DOI: 10.4324/9781003227175-7

COVID-19 is a catalyst for many changes in higher education. The primary effect is to accelerate the digital transformation and the process of crystallization of the new formation of the digital university by transferring the university's activities to the virtual sphere. The mission of the university can be implemented through online communication although it is not free from certain limitations related to, for example, the effectiveness of education. There has been an organizational, technological, social and cultural change that allows universities to educate, conduct research and collaborate with the non-academic community online. In the field of didactics, a strategic change is the radical increase in the importance of e-learning and the virtualization of education. Shifting the burden of learning into online forms is associated with key challenges for management and educators. Synchronous systems such as Teams, Zoom, Meet or advanced, specialized LMS platforms are used, giving the possibility of synchronous and asynchronous e-learning and better control over the verification of learning outcomes and the quality of online education. In this area, innovations towards crowdteaching and crowdlearning are progressing rapidly (Estelles-Miguel et al., 2015). The area of science is the development of a network of international and national cooperation, leading to high-value publications and implementations. The conditions for success include rewarding and creating conditions for development for productive researchers, talent management, implementation of incentive systems. The third mission may be the core of the strategy in the case of universities specializing in applied sciences. In Poland, a lot still has to happen in this regard, because the third mission is a marginal part of the university's activities, and the pandemic is not conducive to strengthening ties with the environment of universities. Management of the entire organization should be based on two pillars: professionalization and digitization of universities. Professionalization of university management concerns the education and development of professional groups of managers in the areas of finance (chancellor), academic administration, knowledge management (chief information officer [CIO], chief IT specialists). The digitization and virtualization of universities uses increasingly complex systems for communication, processing, collecting and analysing data, and managing all aspects of university activities.

The educational sector has undergone a profound metamorphosis towards distance learning (Kang, 2021). COVID-19 has forced universities to move to distance learning on a global scale. Until now, experiences in the field of e-learning concerned mainly forms of blended learning, conducted as a supplement to education in contact with academic teachers. Most universities in the world have the programmes necessary for this, although they were, before the pandemic, a margin in relation to traditional forms of education. Before the pandemic, a smaller part of universities based their offer mainly on e-learning. Examples include: Open U, Embry-Riddle Aeronautical University-Worldwide, Temple University, University of Oklahoma, Arizona State University, Western Kentucky University (top five online undergraduate programmes). Online programmes were implemented as a complement to contact education and implemented mainly by groups of e-learning enthusiasts at universities. Usually, the form of asynchronous e-learning dominated, which made it possible to compensate for the poor direct contact with an academic teacher by greater flexibility and availability of educational materials. The dominant technological solutions in Poland are based on the open-source system – Moodle and include e-learning with a very small component of quality management and education process control. Meanwhile, in the best-developed higher education systems, there is a growing tendency to create virtual learning environments, which, in combination with the managed information system, create an e-learning environment control system (managed learning environment). LMS, in turn, allow not only synchronous and asynchronous e-learning, but also quality management and the online learning process. In all these areas of digitization, virtualization and computerization of education and teaching management at universities, the role of crowdsourcing is increasing, which is becoming one of the most important strategies, concepts and methodologies for the digital transformation of higher education (Marcum, 2014).

When assessing the overall impact of the pandemic on higher education, several broader conclusions can be drawn.

- The strategy of most universities is changing towards digitization and computerization. E-learning, remote management, crowdsourcing and research solutions are being implemented rapidly.
- The pace of creation, implementation and adaptation of the university and its stakeholders in terms of innovative concepts and methods of education, among which crowdsourcing plays a key role, is increasing.
- Universities provide e-learning courses using LMS tools. They are attended by staff and students who have excellent competences enabling remote work. In the group of these competences, the role of knowledge of crowdsourcing work methods is growing.
- Education will be dominated by the hybrid model (mixed classes, remote and in contact) and the blended learning model using crowdteaching and crowdlearning.
- Management of didactics at universities increasingly uses information and communication technologies and, following the example of business, implements IT management tools and analyses mass data, which is closely related to the implementation of crowdsourcing innovations.
- The implementation of strategies, structures and the development of organizational cultures focused on digital management and crowdsourcing are accelerating.

6.2 Quality Management in HEI

The educational process is at the core of the university's mission, which is closely related to quality management. Education is also related to the development and implementation of innovations aimed at improving the educational process. Crowdsourcing is also used in innovative processes related to the quality of education (Nkoana, 2016). The teaching mission plays a crucial role in far more higher education institutions than the research mission and the third stream. In a traditional university, the value of quality in education was built into the university's culture and academic ethos. By definition, the elite universities took care of the quality of education through the selection of students at enrolment and in the education process. Mass education has radically changed the approach to the quality of education (Li & Houjun, 2013). The importance of managing the teaching process at the university has become fundamental. The didactic process is shaped through internal and external education quality assurance systems, accreditation, educational rankings, staff development, surveying students, educators and employers, and research on remuneration and employability of graduates (Avralev & Efimova, 2015; Federkeil, 2008). And yet the measures of the university's research performance have developed very quickly in the last two decades. Accounting for the effectiveness of university teaching activities is much slower and it faces many difficulties. Managing the quality of education is an expensive and multidimensional process that requires many perspectives, and in the operational sphere it forces aggregation of many disproportionate indicators (Titov & Tuulik, 2013). Importance of higher education management should be verified by the possibilities of applying the concepts and effective methods and tools for improving the quality of education (Tarí, 2011).

The quality and quality of education are defined in many ways. The most general descriptions of the quality of education lead in several directions:

- The quality of education is the degree of excellence in achieving the goals of education.
- The quality of education is the result of achieving the assumed goals by the educational process.
- The quality of education is acting in accordance with the established norms and standards.
- The quality of education is the level of satisfaction with education perceived by key stakeholders (students, teaching staff, employers) (Kumar et al., 2016).
- The quality of education is the result of effective management of the teaching process.
- The quality of education is the adequacy of graduates' competences for the labour market and measures of their employability and remuneration.
- The quality of education is the adequacy of the implementation of the educational process and commitment to its mission and goals, within the commonly accepted standards of accountability, reliability and honesty.

Using all these ways of understanding the quality of education, it is possible to indicate the possibilities of their implementation with the use of crowdsourcing. It may be useful for achieving the goals and learning outcomes according to specific standards, which will be favourable to the satisfaction of stakeholders. Crowdsourcing can be used for, inter alia, opinion gathering, teaching innovation, gathering good practice in teaching management and employability (Zheng et al., 2019).

There are many different methods of managing the quality of higher education, which reflect the complexity of university teaching activities and the difficulties in improving, assessing and measuring quality:

- quality strategy and policy – building quality into the university's mission (O'Mahony & Garavan, 2012);
- quality system – internal education quality management system (Kalimullin et al., 2016);
- external education quality management systems at the higher level;
- accreditations and industry accreditations – external audits examining the achievement of educational goals (Nigsch & Schenker-Wicki, 2013);
- rankings and ratings – assessment of the university's reputation and prestige according to the following criteria: scientific, didactic or integrated (Blanco-Ramírez & Berger, 2014);
- learning outcomes – verification of learning outcomes and the effectiveness of the teaching methods used (Duque, 2014);
- certifications and licenses – a test of achieving professional standards through external evaluation (Habánik & Jambor, 2014);
- programme evaluations and benchmarking – the result of environmental expert research, used for peer review (Andor & Toth, 2016);
- customer research – student opinion and satisfaction research (Chalaris et al., 2013; Voss et al., 2007);
- total quality management (TQM) and comprehensive quality improvement – implementation of the concept and methods of continuous improvement at the university.

The description of the methods of managing the quality of education at the university is given depending on the management methodology, so the analysis can focus on quality management or relate to the features of university management. The first method assumes the use of methods of creating, implementing and improving the quality system, improving the service system (Roger, 2014), controlling not only processes, but also documentation and defining management responsibility. Part of these processes, to an increasing extent, along with the development of digital transformation, is crowdsourcing used for educational activities, teaching management and collecting opinions (Boons & Stam, 2019; Jiang et al., 2018; Solemon et al., 2013). However, in order to properly select quality management tools in the education industry, it is better to refer to the level of universities. Publications on this topic allow you for highlighting the following methods:

- benchmarking of model solutions,
- management evaluations, audits,
- student evaluations,
- TQM,
- national, external and international accreditations,
- implementing or creating internal or external education quality standards (such as ISO 9001),
- validation of education,
- awards and quality certifications,
- strategic and operational controlling,
- evaluations and consulting with external stakeholders (such as employers).

Becket and Brooks (2006) analysed the application of management methods to care for the quality of education in universities. The analysis shows that the most common sources are Total Quality Management (Cruickshank, 2003; Motwani & Kumar, 1997). Also, thanks to the links with business, reengineering, EFQM, ISO, sustainable scorecard, SERVQUAL and the Malcolm Baldrige award are used.

Business process reengineering, or reengineering, involves a complete change of organizational processes with the use of IT methods. It means restructuring of processes, technology, strategy, organizational culture and finally the entire organization in order to increase its effectiveness and efficiency.

The EFQM Excellence Model, i.e., the EFQM Improvement Model, is a method taken from the business of using nine criteria to evaluate organization improvement processes (Wongrassamee et al., 2003).

ISO standards (ISO 9000) are recognized international standards that enable the use of comparable measurement methods and quality principles simultaneously in various sectors, including higher education. The quality system aims at constant improvement and customer satisfaction.

Balanced Scorecard – a balanced scorecard has been developed and disseminated by consulting. A management system is used, and efficiency is assessed in the following four areas: financial, learning and growth, customer and internal processes.

SERVQUAL is used in higher education and service management to measure customer satisfaction, perception and expectations. We use the method in the following five dimensions: service adequacy, reaction, value, guarantee and empathy (Becket & Brookes, 2006).

The Malcolm Baldrige Award is used to evaluate performance improvement using the following seven criteria:

- focus on the customer and the market;
- knowledge management;

- process management;
- results;
- leadership;
- strategic planning;
- improvement of human resources (Wilson & Collier, 2000).

Jonathan D. Fife analyses the methods of quality management in universities using two models already in use in the USA. They are presented in Table 6.1.

The AQIP criteria are as follows:

- supporting internal processes at the university, aimed at quality assurance,
- defining and adopting the needs of the quality system by stakeholders – staff, administration, managers, students, but also external stakeholders,
- shaping partnership and cooperation relations between key and other stakeholders,
- leadership and communication between internal and external stakeholders,
- planning a continuous improvement process thanks to pro-quality changes,
- supporting students in learning, reaching for new competences, skills and attitudes,
- such assessment, evaluation and motivation of employees that will enable the implementation of changes, as well as operational management of the quality system,
- striving to achieve various other goals.

Table 6.1 Models of quality improvement

Model name	Abbreviation	Origin	Short description
Academic Quality Improvement Project of The Higher Learning Commission of the North Central Association	AQIP	Academic improvement project used by US accreditation committees.	A set of criteria that must be applied together in order for the quality system and culture to function well.
Malcolm Baldrige National Quality Award	Baldrige	Education quality criterion used in the USA to award the best educational programmes.	The implementation of a quality culture is possible while maintaining the 11 quality principles at the university.
Total Quality Management	TQM	Integrated learning quality management derived from business.	Introducing strategies, policies and procedures in the improvement cycle.

Source: Modified (Fife, 2001).

The above model can be characterized in terms of the principles that ensure the functioning of the quality system in universities. It is important to focus the system (focus) on the mission of the university, also recognized by stakeholders. Continuous improvement of competences and involvement of human resources turns out to be the most important. The following plays an important role: readiness to work in various groups, resolving conflicts, the ability to make decisions, using pro-quality methods and achieving consensus thanks to them. According to the next principle, leadership should harmonize the top-down perspective (responsible for strategic and systemic solutions) with the bottom-up perspective (implementation of quality culture through social practices). Another principle refers to continuous learning – group (structural units and the entire university) and individual (students and employees). Learning becomes the most important organizational process necessary to develop the existing potential. Improving human resources would not be possible without reaching for the system of motivating and developing employees (managers, staff and administration), consisting in the systematic use of rewards and motivators for professional development (people). Collaboration between organizational units, entities from the environment and people should be encouraged. The established quality system must not limit possible changes and the creativity of entities – emphasis is placed on organizational flexibility and readiness to introduce changes, enabling the use of opportunities and the elimination of threats (agility). In order to implement and manage systemic pro-quality changes, one should anticipate the directions of changes in the environment. Planning should follow trends related to educational institutions and their stakeholders in terms of foresight. The quality system in the university can work thanks to the systematic and proper evaluation of its functioning. The measurement is intended to obtain current and useful information of a qualitative and quantitative nature. Information you can trust will help you make the right decisions and improve quality. The last principle is the social responsibility of universities, related to the awareness that education works for the benefit of society and to making constant evaluations and taking actions supporting the university's contribution to the creation of the common good (integrity). The set of principles described and applied simultaneously, and the criteria set out above will ensure the development of not only the formal control system, but above all the quality culture at the university. At the same time, a number of characteristics of the AQIP system fit the processes of digital transformation and may encourage the use of the concept and methods of crowdsourcing. It is all about focus, involvement and collaboration.

AQIP is compared to the quality system in the practice of university quality management and accreditation, i.e., the Baldrige Award. The eleven principles of this programme include the following:

- learning-cantered education – education focused on the learning process, development of students' potential, meeting their needs;
- organizational and personal learning – organizational and unit learning – at all levels, organizational units (i.e., teams, departments or institutes), individual units (employees and students) and the entire institution. Learning draws from the social practices of the educational institution, as they are part of the functioning of the organization. What counts is learning outcomes – i.e., changes and the sharing of skills that will help solve organizational problems and constitute a benchmarking practice;
- focus on results and creating value – focusing on results relevant to key stakeholders (for society, staff and students) and creating value;
- agility – sensitivity and flexibility – readiness to quickly meet the needs of students and other stakeholders, as well as to make the necessary changes in the environment;
- focus on the future – focus on the future, monitoring changes, thanks to which it is possible to identify and study the variables that affect the organization and its situation on the market;
- visionary leadership – visionary leadership, based on the concept of activities and a student-oriented organizational climate, as well as on properly exposed values, related to high requirements and expectations;
- managing for innovation – management based on innovation, orientation towards innovation and change, i.e., improving programmes, social services or processes in order to create new values for stakeholders;
- management by fact – management based on facts, decisions depend on the evaluation and measurement of the effectiveness of activities. They are achieved by comparing the effects with those assumed as part of the organizational strategy. Analyse key organizational processes and provide reliable information;
- valuing faculty, staff and partners – appreciating employees, stakeholders, research and teaching staff related to their development, self-improvement and professional satisfaction;
- public responsibility and citizenship – public and civic responsibility, attaching importance to ethics of operations, social responsibility, safety, environmental protection and public health;
- systems perspective – i.e., managing the entire organization by managing its elements to effectively achieve goals. This is possible thanks to the harmonization of mission, vision, processes and organizational values.

Development of crowdsourcing concepts also leads to association of these concepts with solutions rooted in the management of educational quality. This also applies to Malcolm Baldrige's system and reward.

Jonathan D. Fife made a comparison of both models characterized above. He emphasized the role of assessing and measuring the development of a quality culture in managing the quality of education. Information must be reliable, important to the management process and needed to make a decision. Fife has distinguished four basic types of information to measure and evaluate quality. They are described below.

- Baseline data – input data – enabling the assessment of the current position of the organization at a given stage of its development. These data are used to assess the impact of pro-quality measures, which are carried out on the basis of the obtained basic data.
- Process measurement – analysis and measurement of processes, i.e., the analysis of what is taking place and how it is done in terms of improving the quality of the university's operations. Information on processes is usually provided in a qualitative form, they are intended to answer open-ended questions.
- Contextual outcomes or result trend data – data on results and trends obtained over several years thanks to the analysis of output data and measurement of processes.
- Comparison data – comparative data related to other educational institutions, thanks to which a positional comparison is made. They mainly concern activities of universities competing in the same market. The cited author lists three important types of comparative data. The first type is peer group data, i.e., data on other – similar – institutions, related only to the results achieved. Another type is aspirational data - market comparative data, related to information about similar groups of educational entities, i.e., those attracted by research and education funds and students. The last type of data is benchmark measurement, i.e., a comparison with the best practices in the group and the best institutions. This only applies to a specific type of organizational mission (Sułkowski, 2016).

The described methods of managing and improving the quality of education in higher education can be implemented with the use of crowdsourcing. For example, all forms of collecting opinions and consulting universities with stakeholders may take the form of crowdsourcing, where open calls are announced and the opinions of students, teaching staff, administration and external stakeholders are collected, discussed and analysed. As a result, ideas for innovative educational solutions can emerge, which in turn can be consulted, developed and implemented also using crowdsourcing. Thus, the use of the "crowd" concept and methods applies to the stages of: research, strategic planning, as well as implementation and controlling (Hall & Griffy-Brown, 2016; Solemon et al., 2013).

6.3 Crowdsourcing in Higher Education

With regard to educational activities, there are many types of crowdsourcing activities. They concern both: collecting opinions on education, planning and managing didactics and teaching, improving the quality of education, teaching and education methods, as well as financing and budgeting education. Llorente and Morant (2015) indicate four types of crowdsourcing in higher education: crowdlearning, crowdteaching, crowdtuition and crowdfunding.

Crowdlearning is about group learning using project activities. The learning process consists in the implementation of joint projects designed in an open manner for group work of students. Sharing competences between students and the collective development of knowledge and skills allows students to complete project tasks. Crowdlearning quickly gained importance during the COVID-19 pandemic, when there was a forced transition to distance learning. Open tasks and dividing into virtual groups and performing tasks together by students has become a key element of didactic practice in universities (Farasat et al., 2017).

In crowdteaching, lecturers select, collaborate and share resources together by preparing educational materials. In this area, there has also been a rapid development of cooperation, in particular with the use of virtual groups (Recker et al., 2014). The use of crowd in education is perceived as innovation and radical change (Nascimbeni, 2020).

Crowdtuition may take the form of a tuition fee or a dedicated student loan. Often accompanied by a loan, a repayment programme or post-graduate job offer that allows for tuition reimbursement (Agarwal et al., 2021).

Crowdfunding means obtaining funds for universities for the implementation of an educational, scientific or implementation mission and the mechanisms of its settlement (Bouncken et al., 2015; Costa & Huertas, 2016; Huertas & Costa, 2016). It makes it possible to limit the effects of budget cuts on higher education institutions. The challenge is to incorporate crowdfunding into the accountability system. Obtaining financing is often a radical innovative solution (van der Graaf & Veeckman, 2020).

To these concepts, the following can be added: crowdconsulting and crowdadvising, which can mean the processes of consulting, gathering opinions and advising university stakeholders in response to open calls in online groups. Additionally, for training purposes, it is possible to use crowdtraining. Crowdsourcing can be used here for the professional training of educational managers. Crowdtraining is an innovative educational methodology and puts students in contact with the communities of practice. Students participate in online message boards and collaborate with business. Of course, the question arises whether it is worth multiplying these subsequent "crowd" organizational activities. In addition to the existing "crowd-deliberation", we can easily imagine a "crowdmentoring" or "crowdcoaching". It seems, however, that until such activities develop in organizational practice, they remain hypostases, and according to the Occam's razor principle, it is not worth "multiplying beings without need".

To sum up, crowdsourcing is a source of innovations. The range of uses of crowdsourcing in the teaching activities of universities is getting wider. It includes universities, education, teacher development and training, management of didactics and the quality of education, contacts between students and practice, consulting and counselling, collecting opinions, financing and budget optimization. The innovative potential of crowdsourcing methods is great because their implementation is coupled with the development of the digital transformation of universities. The time of the COVID-19 pandemic and the forced implementation of remote didactics and education management strengthened the orientation towards implementing e-learning and crowdsourcing innovations. Implementation of data-based management, information and communication technologies, the development of virtual communities and IT tools for teaching management are conducive to the implementation of new and innovative solutions.

References

Agarwal, V., Panicker, A., Sharma, A., Rammurthy, R., Ganesh, L., & Chaudhary, S. (2021). Crowdsourcing in higher education: Theory and best practices. In R. Lenart-Gansiniec, & J. Chen (Eds.), *Crowdfunding in the public sector* (pp. 127–135). Springer.

Ahmed, V., & Opoku, A. (2022). Technology supported learning and pedagogy in times of crisis: The case of COVID-19 pandemic. *Education and Information Technologies, 27*(1), 365–405.

Andor, G., & Toth, Z. E. (2016). Peer Review of Teaching in Higher Education– A Case Study of a Hungarian University. Conference Proceedings: The Future of Education (p. 421), Padua, Italy.

Avralev, N., & Efimova, I. (2015). University rankings as a tool for assessing the quality of education in the context of globalization. *Asian Social Science, 11*(10), 292–298.

Becket, N., & Brookes, M. (2006). Evaluating quality management in university departments. *Quality Assurance in Education, 14*(2), 123–142.

Blanco-Ramírez, G., & Berger, J. B. (2014). Rankings, accreditation, and the international quest for quality: Organizing an approach to value in higher education. *Quality Assurance in Education, 22*(1), 88–104.

Boons, M., & Stam, D. (2019). Crowdsourcing for innovation: How related and unrelated perspectives interact to increase creative performance. *Research Policy, 48*(7), 1758–1770.

Bouncken, R. B., Komorek, M., & Kraus, S. (2015). Crowdfunding: The current state of research. *International Business & Economics Research Journal, 14*(3), 407–416.

Chalaris, M., Chalaris, I., Skourlas, C., & Tsolakidis, A. (2013). Extraction of rules based on students' questionnaires. *Procedia - Social and Behavioral Sciences, 73*, 510–517.

Costa, T., & Huertas, S. (2016). Creative debate as a tool to empower and create disruptive thinking within learning contexts in a university design environment. *Procedia - Social and Behavioral Sciences, 228*, 413–417.

Cruickshank, M. (2003). Total quality management in the higher education sector: A literature review from an international and Australian perspective. *TQM & Business Excellence, 14*(10), 1159–1167.

Duque, L. C. (2014). A framework for analysing higher education performance: students' satisfaction, perceived learning outcomes, and dropout intentions. *Total Quality Management & Business Excellence, 25*(1–2), 1–21.

Estelles-Miguel, S., Rius-Sorolla, G., Palmer Gato, M., & Albarracín Guillem, J. M. (2015). Crowdsourcing with university students: Exam questions. In F. J. Garrigos-Simon, I. Gil-Pechuán, & S. Estelles-Miguel (Eds.), *Advances in crowdsourcing* (pp. 97–104). Springer.

Farasat, A., Nikolaev, A., Miller, S., & Gopalsamy, R. (2017). Crowdlearning: Towards collaborative problem-posing at scale. Proceedings of the Fourth (2017) ACM Conference on Learning @ Scale (pp. 221–224), Cambridge MA.

Federkeil, G. (2008). Rankings and quality assurance in higher education. *Higher Education in Europe, 33*(2–3), 219–231.

Habánik, J., & Jambor, J. (2014). Implementation and certification of the quality management system at the university. Ponencia, Conferencia *Científica* "Quality and Leading Innovation", Košice, Slovakia.

Hall, O. P. Jr., & Griffy-Brown, C. (2016). Crowdsourcing management education assessment. *Journal of International Technology and Information Management, 25*(2), 83–100.

Huertas, S., & Costa, T. (2016, June 21–23). Creative debate as a tool to empower and create disruptive thinking within learning contexts in a university design environment. *2nd International Conference on Higher Education Advances*, València, Spain.

Fife, J. D. (2001). Qualitative and quantitative measures: One driver of a quality culture. *New Directions for Institutional Research, 2001*(112), 103–105.

Jiang, Y., Schlagwein, D., & Benatallah, B. (2018, June). A review on crowdsourcing for education: state of the art of literature and practice. Pacific Asia Conference on Information Systems (p. 180), Yokohama, Japan.

Kalimullin, A. M., Khodyreva, E., & Koinova-Zoellner, J. (2016). Development of internal system of education quality assessment at a university. *International Journal of Environmental and Science Education, 11*(13), 6002–6013.

Kang, B. (2021). How the COVID-19 pandemic is reshaping the education service. *The Future of Service Post-COVID-19 Pandemic, 1*, 15–36.

Kumar, P., Raju, N. V. S., & Kumar, M. V. (2016). Quality of quality definitions-an analysis. *International Journal of Scientific Engineering and Technology, 5*(3), 142–148.

Li, J., & Houjun, Y. (2013). Towards a frame work of quality management for cooperative higher education. *2013 the International Conference on Education Technology and Information System*. Dordrecht, The Netherlands.

Llorente, R., & Morant, M. (2015). Crowdsourcing in higher education. In F. Garrigos Simon, I. Gil Pechuán, & S. Estelles-Miguel (Eds.), *Advances in crowdsourcing* (pp. 87–95). Springer.

Marcum, D. (2014). The digital transformation of information, education, and scholarship. *International Journal of Humanities and Arts Computing, 8*(supplement), 1–11.

McCormack, T. J., Lemoine, P. A., Waller, R. E., & Richardson, M. D. (2021). Global higher education: Examining response to the COVID-19 pandemic using agility and adaptability. *Journal of Education and Development, 5*(1), 10–16.

Meiler, Y. (2020). Digital transformation, Covid-19 crisis, digital transformation. Managing a Postcovid19 era. *ESCP impact papers* (pp. 171–178). ESCP Research Institute of Management (ERIM).

Motwani, J., & Kumar, A. (1997). The need for implementing total quality management in education. *International Journal of Educational Management, 11*(3), 131–135.

Nascimbeni, F. (2020). Empowering university educators for contemporary open and networked teaching. In D. Burgos (Ed.), *Radical solutions and open science* (pp. 123–134). Springer.

Nigsch, S., & Schenker-Wicki, A. (2013). Shaping performance: Do international accreditations and quality management really help? *Journal of Higher Education Policy and Management, 35*(6), 668–681.

Nkoana, T. H. (2016). E-learning: Crowdsourcing as an alternative model to traditional learning. *2016 International Conference on Advances in Computing and Communication Engineering* (pp. 423–428), Durban, South Africa.

O'Mahony, K., & Garavan, T. N. (2012). Implementing a quality management framework in a higher education organisation: A case study. *Quality Assurance in Education, v20*(n2), 184–200.

Recker, M., Yuan, M., & Ye, L. (2014). Crowdteaching: Supporting teaching as designing in collective intelligence communities. *International Review of Research in Open and Distributed Learning, 15*(4), 138–160.

Roger, E. (Ed.). (2014). *Quality assurance for university teaching*, Open University Press.

Savić, D. (2020). COVID-19 and work from home: Digital transformation of the workforce. *Grey Journal, 16*(2), 101–104.

Solemon, B., Ariffin, I., Din, M. M., & Anwar, R. M. (2013). A review of the uses of crowdsourcing in higher education. *International Journal of Asian Social Science, 3*(9), 2066–2073.

St-Onge, C., Ouellet, K., Lakhal, S., Dubé, T., & Marceau, M. (2022). COVID-19 as the tipping point for integrating e-assessment in higher education practices. *British Journal of Educational Technology, 53*(2), 349–366.

Sułkowski, Ł (2016). *Kultura akademicka: Koniec utopii?* Wydawnictwo Naukowe PWN.

Tarí, J. J. (2011). Research into quality management and social responsibility. *Journal of Business Ethics, 102*(4), 623–638.

Titov, E., & Tuulik, K. (2013). Management of higher education institution: Quality management through value based management. *American International Journal of Contemporary Research, 3*(9), 29–41.

van der Graaf, S., & Veeckman, C. (2020). Sharing economy and government innovation (May 2020). *Technology Innovation Management Review, 10*(5), 3–5.

Voss, R., Gruber, T., & Szmigin, I. (2007). Service quality in higher education: The role of student expectations. *Journal of Business Research, 60*(9), 949–959.

Wilson, D. D., & Collier, D. A. (2000). An empirical investigation of the Malcolm Baldrige national quality award causal model. *Decision Sciences, 31*(2), 361–383.

Wongrassamee, S., Simmons, E. L., & Gardiner, P. D. (2003). Performance measurement tools: The balanced scorecard and The EFQM excellence model. *Measuring Business Excellence, 7*(1), 14–29.

Zheng, M., Cui, L., He, W., Guo, W., & Lu, X. (2019, August). A dynamic difficulty-sensitive worker distribution model for crowdsourcing quality management. *International Conference on Collaborative Computing: Networking, Applications and Worksharing* (pp. 12–27), London, UK.

Conclusion

This book deals with and combines two important issues from the point of view of higher education institutions: innovation and crowdsourcing. Firstly, innovations, in particular digital innovations, in higher education are perceived to result from changes in the regional and economic contexts in which higher education institutions are embedded and the changing nature of public policies with their coercive effects on the internal organization of universities. These changes are a response to the demands of digital transformation, rapid social development and technological and economic changes. In this approach, innovations play a key role – they contribute to the success and development of the organization, creating positive value, shaping the right attitudes towards the organization, including the ability to learn and adapt to a changing environment, improving the quality of services, customer and employee satisfaction, improving the image of the organization and attracting new cooperation partners.

Secondly, the necessity of cooperation of higher education with the environment is stressed as it was emphasized in the UNESCO declaration, which should come down to the implementation of the postulates of openness and transparency of universities, establishing relations with the environment and involving higher education in solving problems. Collaboration with online communities can be a natural consequence of these guidelines. In this approach, crowdsourcing gains importance, in particular, due to its potential for not only simultaneous acquisition of resources from many sources of human knowledge that are outside the organization, but also customer engagement, innovation and increasing institutional legitimacy. Moreover, the use of appropriate crowdsourcing techniques in higher education can increase the efficiency of learning processes and optimize curricula that lead to better achievement by the university management and its employees. In addition, crowdsourcing allows for the improvement and introduction of a number of innovations in educating students.

Crowdsourcing promoters in higher education institutions are convinced that it can be useful for gaining ideas, opinions, feedback from the virtual

DOI: 10.4324/9781003227175-8

community, gaining support for various projects, as well as improving communication between individual stakeholders, and even collecting data as part of scientific research, creating textbooks and raising funds for educational projects. In the case of the latter, it is indicated that the use of crowdsourcing enables optimization of the institution's budget and a more effective use of time for learning.

In each chapter, we show that crowdsourcing is important from the point of view of higher education institutions. We prove that crowdsourcing in higher education contributes to reduction and optimization of costs, exchange of materials, creation of textbooks, conducting research, sharing knowledge and obtaining ideas for development or funding for scholarships for students, sports teams, research projects of students, researchers or study trips. Of course, the examples of crowdsourcing used in the university related environment differ in scale, range and type from one case to another. Nevertheless, it can be indicated that all types of crowdsourcing are implemented at universities: collective intelligence, value creation by the crowd, gathering opinions and raising funds. Crowdfunding projects and those related to collecting analytical data predominate.

However, when implementing crowdsourcing at a university, one cannot forget about the specific needs and conditions of operation of this type of an entity. Poorly managed crowdsourcing may cause dissatisfaction of the virtual community with the mere participation in the crowdsourcing initiative, which may contribute to discouragement and dissatisfaction as well as negative perception of the fundraiser initiator. In addition, crowdsourcing may generate excessive costs with a decrease in the performance of virtual community members in relation to that of experts. Finally, a university may obtain low-quality solutions, while the cost of engaging a virtual community may drain resources from professional administrative work. Crowdsourcing can also limit innovation as creating ideas takes time and crowdsourcing focuses on speed. Moreover, group creativity requires colleagues to know each other, which is difficult in the case of members of virtual communities.

Bearing in mind the considerations in individual chapters of this book, it can be assumed that despite the fears and the need to manage the crowdsourcing initiative – crowdsourcing is not only a challenge, but also a necessity for universities and may become a complementary part of formal education. Consequently, crowdsourcing may become a new paradigm for developing educational innovation in the next few years. We believe that the knowledge on the use of crowdsourcing for innovation in higher education institutions is still far from complete. In particular, research is needed on the possibility of using crowdsourcing in the vocational training of educational managers. The literature indicates that such a scope of crowdsourcing application may contribute to the optimization of obtaining results, the rational use of knowledge, skills, experience and interests of the virtual community, creating new favourable conditions for establishing effective communication with Internet users, engaging an active community in participating in the process of forming collegiate bodies and streamlining management decisions. In particular, the latter is a challenge and a priority for higher education. In the face of COVID-19, there was a need for greater cooperation with widely understood stakeholders and the implementation of innovative management and education solutions.

Index

Note: Page numbers in "**bold**" indicate the tables.

abilities 36
academic crowdsourcing 16; *see also* crowdsourcing
Afuah, A. 49
agile 8
Agile Manifesto 8
agile organization 9
agility 7, 103
Alavi, M. 85
AQIP criteria 101, **102–103**
Aris, H. 51
artificial intelligence 10, 39, 40
augmented reality 40

balanced scorecard (BSC) 81, 100
Bartolini, C. **57**
baseline data 104
Becket, N. 100
"Behemoths" 10
big data 39
big data analytics (BDA) 8
blue ocean strategy 10
"Borsa Parole" 74
Brabham, D. C. 49, 55, **56**, 59–61
Britannica encyclopaedia 6
broadcast search 60
Brookes, M. 100
Bryer, T. A. 63
bureaucratization of university 22
Burger-Helmchen, T. **58**
business intelligence (BI) IT systems 86, 88
business model innovation 33–34
business performance management (BPM) 88
business process management system (BPMS) 88

California State University 73
Castells, M. 5–6
causal knowledge 83; *see also* knowledge
cause-and-effect understanding 83
Challenge.gov 63
Chen, J. 32
Chesbrough, H. 33
cloud computing 8, 15, 40, 44, 86
co-creating knowledge 85; *see also* knowledge
Columbia University 73
comparison data 104
competences: concept of 36; defined 36; digital 36–37; effective actions 36; *see also* abilities; knowledge; skills
computer-aided design (CAD) 89
computer applications 6
computerized administration 43
computer networks 6
computer simulation 41
conditional knowledge 84; *see also* knowledge
conscious innovation management 41–42; *see also* management
contextual outcomes 104
Cooper, T. L. 63
Corney, J. R. **56**, **57**
corporate performance management (CPM) 88
COVID-19 pandemic 2; digitization in 95; distance learning in universities 96; impact on innovations in HEI 95–97; remote activities in universities in 14; *see also* post-COVID HEI
creativity 33, 48, 61, 63, 71, 102, 110

Index   113

crowd: capital 61; casting 55; content 59; creation 55; crowdsourcer 53; knowledge discovery and management 59; learning 60, 96, 105; members 59; organizational activities 105; role of 53; storming 59; support 59; teaching 60; tuition 60; voting 59; wisdom of 52, 55
crowdadvising 105
crowd-based digital innovation 39
crowdcoaching 105
crowdconsulting 105
crowd-deliberation 105
crowdfunding 59, 60, 75–77, 105
crowdmentoring 105
crowdsourcer 53
crowdsourcing: academic 16; components of 51–54; concept of 48–51; conviction 2; in crisis management 2; defined 1, 49–50; as a driver of innovations 70–72; of educational research efforts 2; essence of 48–51; external and internal 60; HEI 70–77; importance for education 1; innovation and 95–106; internal 60, 64, 72–73; knowledge and 89–91; in learning and teaching processes 44–45; for new ideas 73; for new services 73–75; for new solution 75; organizations 1–2; platform 54, 71; potential of 2; promoters 45, 109–110; propagators of 70; teaching 90; trends 61–63; typology of 55–61, **56–58**; use of 1–2; work–internal 60
Crowdsourcing (Brabham) 49
crowdteaching 96, 105
crowdtraining 105
crowdtuition 105
customer relationships management (CRM) 89
cybernetic organization management model 11
cyber-physical systems 40

data-based decision-making systems 5, 18, 22, 82
data literacy 37
Davenport University 75
Dawson, R. **57**
decision-making 42; data-based 5, 18, 22, 82; evidence-based 17, 82
declared knowledge 83; *see also* knowledge

dematerializing credentials 41
De Vries, A. P. 52
didactic process 98
digital: breakthrough 12–13; capability 36–39; collaboration 38; communication 38; competences 36–37; consumers 6–7; creation 37–38; disruption 12–13; economy 4–8, 37; educational resources engine 41; identity 38–39; learning 38; management methods 9; participation 38; revolution 4–8; tools 11; wellbeing 38–39
Digital Education Action Plan 34
digital innovations 37–38; *see also* innovation
digital orientation 34–36; *see also* strategic orientation
digital technologies 5; adaptation of 8; in organization 8, 10
digital transformation: complexity of 7; defined 12–14; digital economy 4–8; digital revolution 4–8; digital university 14–22; digitization 4–8; of higher education 12–14; organizations 8–12; of societies 7–8; technologies 5; of universities 12; virtualization 4–8
digital university: development of 14; management of 14–22
digitization 4–8, 80, 90; concept of 4; in COVID-19 pandemic 95; defined 4; negative aspects of 6; organizational boundaries 7; of organizations 39; of products/services 12; of societies and people 14; of society 4, 11; of technology 36; of universities 22, 96–97
distributed human-intelligence tasking 60
Doan, A. **58**
Drucker, P. F. 33
Dutil, P. 62

economy: digital 4–8, 37; knowledge-based 5, 71; network 5, 7
education: crowdsourcing importance for 1; higher 12–14; hybridization of 17; innovation in 34; intelligent 43; learning-cantered 103; quality of 98–99; smart 43; *see also* higher education; higher education institutions (HEI)
EFQM Excellence Model 100
EFQM Improvement Model 100
e-learning systems 15, 17, 86, 96–97

elite universities 98; *see also* universities
enterprise content management 89; *see also* management
enterprise performance management (EPM) 88
enterprise resource planning (ERP) 89
entrepreneurial universities 15, 18; *see also* universities
entrepreneurship orientation 35
Estellés-Arolas, E. 50–51, 55, **58**, 59, 89
evidence-based decision making 17, 82
explicit knowledge 83; *see also* knowledge

Faust, D. 51
Fife, Jonathan D. 101, 103–104
Fourier, C. 6
Freeman, C. 33
French encyclopaedists 6
Fuchs-Kittowski, F. 51

"gafas" 10
Geerts, S. **57**
Geiger, D. 51, **58**
Generation Education 75
GiveCampus 76
globalization of science 16
González-Ladrónde-Guevara, F. 50–51, 55, **58**, 89
"The Great War Archive" 73
Guittard, C. **58**
Gummesson 50

higher education: challenges 1; crowdsourcing in 2, 104–106; digital transformation of 12–14; practices 72–75; *see also* education
higher education institutions (HEI) 1, 2–3; crowdsourcing in 70–77; employees 72; innovations in 39–45, 70–72; knowledge management 80–91; managers/leaders 42; possibilities of crowdfunding 75–77; quality management in 97–104; supervision of 18
homogenization of data 39
Hosseini, M. 51
Howe, J. 49, 55, **56**, 59
human capital management 16
human-intelligence tasking, distributed 60
human resource management 82
Humboldt-type university 19
hybridization of education 17
hyperconnectivity 8

Industry and Society 4.0 concept 11
information and communication technologies (ICT) 8, 9, 15; development and implementation of 9–10; in knowledge in HEI 86–89; knowledge management methods 80; management processes 10; market role of 10; proficiency 37
information literacy 37
information technologies 80
InnoCentive platform 52
innovation: business model 33–34; categorization 33; crowdsourcing and 95–106; defined 32–33; digital capability 36–39; digital orientation 34–36; drivers and barriers of 41–43; in education systems 34; in HEI 39–45; in knowledge 80–91; marketing 33; process 34; product 33; service 33–34; trends in 43–45
"Innovation Station" project 75
input data 104
intelligent education 43
internal crowdsourcing 60, 64, 72–73
Internet: audience 52; community 52, 59–60, 61; principle of inequality 53; technologies 5
Internet of Everything 8
Internet of Things (IoT) 4, 8, 10–11, 39, 43–44
ISO standards 100
ITC 11

Jeppesen, L. B. 52

Kantola, J. 50
Kazai, G. 53
Kleeman, F. **56**
knowledge 36; causal 83; co-creating 85; conditional 84; crowdsourcing and 89–91; declared 83; discovery and management 59; explicit 83; individual *versus* social dichotomy 83; information and communication technologies in 86–89; innovation in 80–91; management 80–91; in organizations 80–81; procedural 83; relational 84; social 83; socialization of 83; sources of 85; tacit 82–83; taxonomies of **84**; types of 82–84; *see also* education; higher education
knowledge-based economy 5, 71; *see also* economy

knowledge management (KM): goals for 81; higher education institutions (HEI) 80–91; methods and concepts used in **88**; overview 80–81; paradigms in 85–86; perspectives of **87**; in private and public sectors 82; in universities 82, 86
Kotarbiński, T. 85
Kowalska, M. 51

Lakhani, K. R. 52
Lars 51
"Latest Polish vocabulary" project 74
learning: crowd 60, 96; crowdsourcing in 44–45; digital 38; distance 96; education 103; e-learning systems 15, 17, 86, 96–97; online distributed learning environments 2; organizational and personal 103; orientation 35; smart learning environment 44
lecturers 44
Leidner, D. E. 85
Llorente, R. 60, 105
logos 49
Ludwig and Maximilian University in Munich 74

Malcolm Baldrige Award 100
management: business performance management (BPM) 88; business process management system (BPMS) 88; conscious innovation 41–42; corporate performance management (CPM) 88; crowdsourcing in crisis 2; customer relationships management (CRM) 89; cybernetic organization management model 11; digital management methods 9; of digital university 14–22; enterprise content 89; enterprise performance management (EPM) 88; by fact 103; knowledge 59, 80–91; organizations 9; processes 10; professionalization of 18; quality management in HEI 97–104; total quality management (TQM) 88, 99–100; university 86–88; *see also* knowledge management (KM)
Mansfield, E. 32
marketing innovation 33; *see also* innovation
market orientation 35
massive online open classes (MOOC) 40
media literacy 37

Mergel, I. 63
The Meta Data Games project 74
"Metropolitalia" project 74
"Microryza" platform 75–76
mobile applications 6
modern digital technologies 43
Morant, M. 60, 105
multimodal literacy 37

native speakers 74
NBIC (nano-bio-info-cogno) technologies 9
network cooperation 7
network economy 5, 7
networking 7
network market 5
network revolution 6
network society 5–6
network technologies 48
new innovation model 62
non-public universities 18

online civic communication channel 59
online communities 52, 59, 60, 71
online distributed learning environments 2
online transaction processing 89
open Internet communities 6; *see also* network society
openness 90
open science 16
organization(s): behaviour of 35; of digital age 8–12; digital transformation 8–12; management 9; network methods of 11; strategic orientation 35; use of crowdsourcing 1–2; virtualization 9
organizational and personal learning 103
organizational strategy 10
Organization for Economic Co-operation and Development (OECD) 32
Oslo Manual 32–33
ostentatious consumption 6
Owen, R. 6

peer-vetted creative production 60
Pénin, J. **58**
personal/professional development 38
Poland 96, 97
Polanyi, M. 82
post-COVID HEI 95–106; *see also* COVID-19 pandemic

procedural knowledge 83; *see also* knowledge
process innovation 34; *see also* innovation
process measurement 104
product co-creation 7
product innovation 33; *see also* innovation
professionalization 96
project portfolio management (PPM) 88
public responsibility and citizenship 103

quality improvement models **101**
quality management in HEI 97–104; *see also* higher education institutions (HEI)
quasi-corporate systems 16
Quinton, S. 35

Reddy, S. K. 6
reengineering 9–10
Reinartz, W. 6
relational knowledge 84
reprogrammability 39
responsiveness 7
result trend data 104
Rheingold, H. 52
Rouse, A. C. **57**

Saint-Simon, H. de 6
Salem State crowdfunding 75–76
"Saluki App" project 75
ScaleFunder 77
Schenk, E. **58**
scholarship 37–38
Schumpeter, J. 32
sector analysis 81
self-assessment tests 41
self-referential nature of digital technology 39
service innovation 33, 34, 71
SERVQUAL 100
Sivula, A. 50
skills 36
SMACIT 4
smart campus 44
smart classroom 43
smart education 43
smart learning environment 44
smart teachers 44
smart university 43–44
socialism 6
social knowledge 83
social networks 6, 52

software model understood as a service (Software-as-a-Service – Saas) 8
strategic maps 81
strategic orientation 35; *see also* digital orientation
structural changes 12
supplier relationships management 89
synchronous systems 96
systems perspective 103

tacit knowledge 82–83
"Takeashine" project 75
teaching crowdsourcing 90
technological leader 11
technologies 11; coupling 7; digital transformation 12; digitization of 36; educational 2–3; information 80; Internet 5; NBIC 9; network 48; self-referential nature of digital 39; *see also* crowdsourcing; digital; digitization; information and communication technologies (ICT); Internet of Things (IoT)
"Tech Support" 74
third-generation universities 17
Times Higher Educational Awards 74
total quality management (TQM) 88, 99–100
Transcribe Europeana 1914-1918 74
Tucci, C. L. 49

UNED University in Spain 73
UNESCO 109
universities: administration of 18; bureaucratization of 22; characteristics of 22; commercialization and corporatization of 19; digital innovations 40; distance learning 96; elite 98; entrepreneurial 15, 18; financing of 18; flexibility of 17; four waves of 14–15, 18–19, **20–21**; fundamental mission of 19; Humboldt-type 19; management systems 86–88; non-public 18; professionalization of 19, 96; remote activities 14; staff 17–18; third-generation 17
University of Essex Click 76
University of Notre Dame 74
University of Oxford 73–74
University of Southern Illinois in Carbondale 75
University of Utah 75
USEED 77

Vakkari, P. 54
value co-creation 7
Van Dijk, J. A. 5–6
Veblen, T. 6
virtual: campuses 15; communities 2, 5, 45, 52, 53, 62–63, 70, 72–73, 110; learning environments 97; methods and tools in organization 9; prediction of real cases 41; reality 40; research teams 15
virtualization 4–8, 9, 95–97

visionary leadership 103
Vukovic, M. 54, **56**, **57**
Vuurens, J. B. 52

web applications 6
work–internal crowdsourcing 60

Yin, X. 32

Zhao, Y. 51, 54
Zhu, Q. 51, 54